LOST CIVILIZATIONS

THE ETRUSCANS

Other titles in the *Lost Civilizations* series include:

LOST CIVILIZATIONS

THE
ETRUSCANS

Don Nardo

LUCENT BOOKS
An imprint of Thomson Gale, a part of The Thomson Corporation

THOMSON
GALE

Detroit • New York • San Francisco • San Diego • New Haven, Conn. • Waterville, Maine • London • Munich

LIBRARY OF CONGRESS CATALOGING-IN-PUBLICATION DATA

Nardo, Don, 1947–
    The Etruscans / by Don Nardo.
      p. cm. — (Lost civilizations)
    Includes bibliographical references and index.
    ISBN 1-59018-564-1 (hardcover : alk. paper)
    1. Etruscans—Juvenile literature. I. Title. II. Series: Lost civilizations (San Diego, Calif.)
    DG223.N35 2004
    937'.501—dc22
                                                          2004021595

Printed in the United States of America

CONTENTS

FOREWORD

"What marvel is this?" asked the noted eighteenth-century German poet and philosopher, Friedrich Schiller. "O earth . . . what is your lap sending forth? Is there life in the deeps as well? A race yet unknown hiding under the lava?" The "marvel" that excited Schiller was the discovery, in the early 1700s, of two entire ancient Roman cities buried beneath over sixty feet of hardened volcanic ash and lava near the modern city of Naples, on Italy's western coast. "Ancient Pompeii is found again!" Schiller joyfully exclaimed. "And the city of Hercules rises!"

People had known about the existence of long lost civilizations before Schiller's day, of course. Stonehenge, a circle of huge, very ancient stones had stood, silent and mysterious, on a plain in Britain as long as people could remember. And the ruins of temples and other structures erected by the ancient inhabitants of Egypt, Palestine, Greece, and Rome had for untold centuries sprawled in magnificent profusion throughout the Mediterranean world. But when, why, and how were these monuments built? And what were the exact histories and beliefs of the peoples who built them? A few scattered surviving ancient literary texts had provided some partial answers to some of these questions. But not until Pompeii and Herculaneum started to emerge from the ashes did the modern world begin to study and re-

construct lost civilizations in a systematic manner.

Even then, the process was at first slow and uncertain. Pompeii, a bustling, prosperous town of some twenty thousand inhabitants, and the smaller Herculaneum met their doom on August 24, A.D. 79, when the nearby volcano, Mt. Vesuvius, blew its top and literally erased them from the map. For nearly seventeen centuries, their contents, preserved in a massive cocoon of volcanic debris, rested undisturbed. Not until the early eighteenth century did people begin raising statues and other artifacts from the buried cities; and at first this was done in a haphazard, unscientific manner. The diggers, who were seeking art treasures to adorn their gardens and mansions, gave no thought to the historical value of the finds. The sad fact was that at the time no trained experts existed to dig up and study lost civilizations in a proper manner.

This unfortunate situation began to change in 1763. In that year, Johann J. Winckelmann, a German librarian fascinated by antiquities (the name then used for ancient artifacts), began to investigate Pompeii and Herculaneum. Although he made some mistakes and drew some wrong conclusions, Winckelmann laid the initial, crucial groundwork for a new science—archaeology (a term derived from two Greek words meaning "to talk about ancient things"). His book, *History of the Art of Antiquity*, became a model for the first generation of archaeologists to follow in their efforts to understand other lost civilizations. "With unerring sensitivity," noted scholar C.W. Ceram explains, "Winckelmann groped toward original insights, and expressed them with such power of language that the cultured European world was carried away by a wave of enthusiasm for the antique ideal. This . . . was of prime importance in shaping the course of archaeology in the following century. It demonstrated means of understanding ancient cultures through their artifacts."

In the two centuries that followed, archaeologists, historians, and other scholars began to piece together the remains of lost civilizations around the world. The glory that was Greece, the grandeur that was Rome, the cradles of human civilization in Egypt's Nile valley and Mesopotamia's Tigris-Euphrates valley, the colorful royal court of ancient China's Han Dynasty, the mysterious stone cities of the Maya and Aztecs in Central America—all of these

and many more were revealed in fascinating, often startling, if sometimes incomplete detail by the romantic adventure of archaeological research. This work, which continues, is vital. "Digs are in progress all over the world," says Ceram. "For we need to understand the past five thousand years in order to master the next hundred years."

Each volume in the *Lost Civilizations* series examines the history, works, everyday life, and importance of ancient cultures. The archaeological discoveries and methods used to gather this knowledge are stressed throughout. Where possible, quotes by the ancients themselves, and also by later historians, archaeologists, and other experts support and enliven the text. Primary and secondary sources are carefully documented by footnotes and each volume supplies the reader with an extensive Works Consulted list. These and other research tools afford the reader a thorough understanding of how a civilization that was long lost has once more seen the light of day and begun to reveal its secrets to its captivated modern descendants.

INTRODUCTION

LIFTING THE VEIL OF MYSTERY

The Etruscans were a vibrant and highly accomplished people who inhabited large sections of Italy in the first millennium B.C. Here is what one of the leading historians of the early twentieth century said about them in 1944:

> [In 1200 B.C., the Etruscans] still lived in the Near East and had not yet migrated westward. . . . Some of the Etruscans settled in the Greek islands. . . . [Later, in Italy] the fears of the Latin tribes [including the Romans] regarding an invasion of the Etruscans were realized. . . . [The] Etruscan kings soon extended their power over the Latin tribes. . . . Thus, Rome became a city-kingdom under an Etruscan king, like the other Etruscan cities . . . and such it remained for two and a half centuries. . . . The civilization of Rome became essentially Etruscan.[1]

It is a tribute to the hard work of archaeologists and the intrinsic value of archaeology as a science that every point made in the preceding paragraph has since been shown to be either incorrect or exaggerated and misleading. First, the vast majority of scholars now think that the Etruscans were indigenous to Italy, not migrants from the Near East. In this scenario, the Stone Age

and Bronze Age inhabitants of Etruria, the northern Italian region now called Tuscany, eventually developed into the people whom others called the Etruscans. (In contrast, the Etruscans called themselves the Rasenna.)

Second, the idea of a forceful Etruscan invasion, takeover, and military occupation of Rome has been strongly disputed, if not totally discarded. Experts do accept that a few of Rome's early kings were Etruscan and that early Roman culture was strongly influenced by that of its Etruscan neighbors. But it is now generally believed that this was a largely peaceful, voluntary process; the less culturally advanced Romans allowed themselves to be partially "Etruscanized," yet remained essentially an independent Latin city. In addition, many other widely held assumptions about the Etruscans have had to be rethought in light of the steady emergence of new evidence.

The Nature of the Evidence

There are two major reasons why it is not surprising that modern scholars got so much about the Etruscans wrong for so long. The first involved attitudes and methodology within the scholarly community itself. Well into the twentieth century, a majority of historians viewed the evidence produced by archaeology, the physical excavation of past cultures, as second-rate. Or at least they saw it as only supplementary to the surviving ancient written sources, which they considered primary. As noted scholars Graeme Barker and Tom Rasmussen explain:

> There was a time, not so long ago, when the relationship between history and archaeology could be characterized—or at least caricatured—as simple: archaeology was an expensive way of telling historians what they knew already . . . and if it indicated anything at variance with the written sources, it was obviously wrong! . . . More recently, as the two disciplines have learned to work more closely together, historians and archaeologists have tended to describe the relationship as equal. . . . Many scholars would say that . . . history and archaeology are more a single study of the human past than different approaches to it. All our sources, whether written records . . .

A dinner party is depicted in this wall painting from the Tomb of the Leopards at the Etruscan city of Tarquinii. Most evidence for the Etruscans comes from tombs.

or excavated data, are "archaeology" in the sense that they comprise a single source of material culture that has survived . . . from the past.[2]

The second major reason that scholars long misread the evidence about the Etruscans was the amount and nature of that evidence. To begin with, it was (and remains) relatively scarce, especially when compared with the large volume of surviving evidence for the Greeks and Romans who lived during the same time period as

One of the few surviving Etruscan portrait busts depicts an unidentified individual.

the Etruscans. The reasons for this paucity of evidence are fairly well understood. First, the Etruscan language has not yet been fully deciphered. And even if this were to happen tomorrow, the net gain would be small, since only a few, mostly short examples of Etruscan writing have been found. There are no ancient Etruscan chronicles or histories, therefore. So most of the leading characters and events of Etruscan history are virtually unknown.

There is also the problem of what archaeologists call "overbuilding." Simply put, the sites of many of the Etruscan towns were so strategic and well chosen that they were never abandoned. After the demise of Etruscan civilization, the Romans and both medieval and modern Europeans erected new habitations directly atop the older ones. So a majority of Etruscan ruins and artifacts lie buried deep beneath several layers of habitation, including modern city streets and houses. And few, if any, of the present-day residents are willing to have their homes and neighborhoods bulldozed in the cause of advancing historical knowledge.

As for those Etruscan ruins that have survived in accessible areas, the great majority are old tombs, which most later peoples chose not to overbuild. Yet what was not buried by human progress fell prey to human greed. The vast majority of the Etruscan burial places were looted of most of their contents in either ancient or modern times. (One modern Italian tomb robber, Luigi Perticarari, made a handsome living by hawking the objects he personally stole from some four thousand Etruscan grave sites.) Thus, archaeologists and historians have had to try to piece together a coherent picture of an entire civilization based in

Vegetation chokes the exterior of an ancient underground tomb, one of many found near the Etruscan city of Caere.

large part on the few artifacts that thieves and natural forces have left intact.

Yet even if surviving Etruscan writings and artifacts are fragmentary, what about the writings of other ancient peoples *about* the Etruscans? The fact is that the Etruscans did not develop in isolation. Rather, they were profoundly influenced by the Greeks, with whom they long interacted. And in their turn, the Etruscans had just as profound an impact on the Romans, who eventually absorbed the Etruscan people and their lands. Surely, one would hope, the Greeks and Romans must have recorded important facts about a people who had once controlled large sections of the Italian peninsula. Unfortunately, however, this is not the case. Although the Greeks and Ro-

mans did write about the Etruscans, those tracts that have survived are largely superficial, unkind or mean-spirited, highly biased, or all of these. Noted and prolific historian Michael Grant explains:

The surviving Greek and Latin works that deal with the Etruscans tend to do so in a cursory fashion, and only when their concerns happen to impinge in some way or other upon Greek or Roman affairs. And even then, for the most part, the treatment given by these writers is sketchy and ignorant, and above all, suffers frequently, and indeed almost invariably, from the injection of hostile prejudices.[3]

Stone and terra-cotta coffins crowd an Etruscan tomb dating from the fourth century B.C. *It was customary to depict the dead on coffin lids.*

Raising a Lost People from Obscurity

As a result of all these problems, for a long time most books and articles about the Etruscans invariably referred to them as "mysterious" or "enigmatic." As late as 1984, a popular coffee-table book about ancient civilizations called them "the elusive Etruscans," who "remain among the most mysterious of lost civilizations."[4]

Fortunately, however, the veil of mystery enshrouding the Etruscans and their influential culture is steadily, if slowly, lifting. Authorities in a number of Italian towns are allowing limited excavations at selected urban sites. These digs are yielding new artifacts that provide small but valuable snap-

shots of Etruscan life. Meanwhile, a resurgence of interest in the Etruscans in recent years has led to a larger number of Etruscan excavations than ever before. As a result, roads, ports, farms, fortifications, and other aspects of Etruscan civilization that have long lain buried in the countryside are coming to light. Improved archaeological techniques help to reveal these sites, as well as more Etruscan tombs. Special drills tunnel down into the tombs, and researchers lower miniaturized cameras through the holes to see if what is inside is worth digging up.

In addition, an Etruscan mining town that had not been overbuilt by later structures was recently discovered. Called Accesa (after a nearby lake), it lies near the modern Italian town of Massa Marittima, in southern Tuscany. Several acres have been unearthed so far and have revealed actual Etruscan houses and streets. The site has so much potential for expanding knowledge about its builders that many people have come to call it the "Etruscan Pompeii" (in reference to the famous Roman town that was buried by a volcanic eruption, which, fortunately for modern investigators, preserved much of its contents intact).

Finally, scholars are also closely examining and reevaluating existing Etruscan artifacts. As they learn more about this fascinating ancient people, they often find that objects unearthed long ago take on new and unexpected meanings. Coordination of both new and old finds and theories is also improving. In March 2003, Etruscologists (experts on the Etruscans) from around the world met to compare notes at the University of Pennsylvania Museum of Archaeology in Philadelphia. More such gatherings are planned for the future. In addition, well-publicized museum shows of Etruscan artifacts became common in Europe and North America in the 1980s, and in the words of ancient art historian Nigel Spivey, "the momentum of exhibitions shows no sign yet of slowing."[5] Spivey and other scholars hope that continued excavations, studies, and exhibitions will further raise one of the greatest civilizations of the ancient world from centuries of neglect and obscurity.

CHAPTER ONE

ORIGINS AND DEVELOPMENT OF ETRUSCAN CULTURE

One reason the Etruscans were long seen as mysterious was that their origins were largely unknown. Many ancient writers had said that they came to Italy from somewhere in the exotic "East," likely Asia Minor (what is now Turkey), in some long-forgotten age. And the majority of early modern scholars simply accepted this theory without much critical questioning. Such acceptance naturally raised many questions that were difficult to answer. For instance, where exactly in the East had the Etruscans originated? Why did they migrate to Italy and when? Did they subjugate or merge with the native inhabitants of Etruria, the northern Italian region that came to be named after them?

More than a century of painstaking archaeological work has shown that these questions are essentially meaningless because the theory that spawned them is almost certainly wrong. Once scholars accepted that the Etruscans were native Italians, they became far less mysterious. (This is not to say that they have been completely demystified by any means. Much about their civilization remains unknown or unclear.) Archaeologists had already discerned some basic facts about the early history of Etruria, including its prehistoric stages and initial contacts with the Greeks and other outsiders. This information could now be applied directly to the Etruscans. In other words, the early inhabitants of Etruria and the early Etruscans are now seen as one and the same.

Origins in Asia Minor?

The dispute over and mystery surrounding the origins of the Etruscans were not new to the modern age. In fact, ancient Greek and Roman scholars held this very same debate about the Etruscans who dwelled in their midst. Most of these ancient scholars advocated the theory of eastern origins, but a handful believed that the Etruscans were indigenous to Italy. It is interesting that early modern scholars were divided on the issue along similar lines. This demonstrates how their placing too much trust in and reliance on the written sources (as opposed to the archaeological data) led them astray. Most of the ancient assertions about Etruscan origins were evidently based on legend and hearsay. And in their eagerness to accept these accounts at face value, many early modern scholars needlessly perpetuated the mystery.

The first of these ancient accounts—which is also the very first literary mention of the Etruscans in Western literature—was that of the eighth-century B.C. Greek poet

Hesiod in his *Theogony*. In this epic poem about the origins of the world and the gods, Hesiod did not directly address the question of Etruscan origins. Rather, he briefly described them as living in "the midst of the holy islands," located "so far away."[6] It is possible that he meant Italy and its immediate environs, because in his day Italy, Sicily, and Sardinia were still somewhat ill defined, exotic places lying in the sea far to the west of Greece. However, it is now impossible to figure out exactly what Hesiod meant. And in any case, he likely did not know any more about the Etruscans than he said.

One pertinent element of Hesiod's account is that he calls the Etruscans the Ty-rsenians. This was one of several names used by the Greeks and Romans to describe the people who called themselves the Rasenna and are now known as the Etruscans. Another name was the Tyrrheni, or Tyrrhenians. The latter term has survived, as the waters lying off Italy's western coast, where Etruscan sailors once held sway, are still referred to as the Tyrrhenian Sea. Other ancient names for the Etruscans included the more familiar Etrusci and Tusci (for which the region known both as Etruria and Tuscany is named).

Whatever the Greeks and Romans chose to call the Etruscans, in the fifth century B.C. Greek writers began to talk about their

An Etruscan husband and wife are depicted in terra-cotta on a coffin lid found in one of the tombs at Caere.

The fifth-century B.C. *Greek historian Herodotus reads from his* Histories. *In the book, Herodotus speculates about the origin of the Etruscans.*

origins. The most famous account was that of the historian Herodotus, who hailed from Halicarnassus, a Greek city on the western coast of Asia Minor. In his *Histories*, he said that the Etruscans were originally natives of Lydia, a prosperous kingdom encompassing much of west-central Asia Minor. The Lydians, Herodotus wrote,

claim to have invented the games [dice, knucklebones, ball games] which are now commonly played both by themselves and by the Greeks. These games are supposed to have been invented at the time when they sent a colony to settle in Tyrrhenia [i.e., Etruria]. . . . The king divided the pop-

16

ulation into two groups and determined by drawing lots which should emigrate and which should remain at home. He appointed himself to rule [those who would stay] and his son, Tyrrhenus, to command the emigrants. The lots were drawn, and one [group] went down to the coast . . . where they built vessels, put aboard all their household effects, and sailed in search of a livelihood elsewhere. They passed many countries and finally reached Umbria, in the north of Italy, where they settled and still live to this day.[7]

Herodotus added that the travelers changed their name from Lydians to Tyrrhenians in honor of their leader, Tyrrhenus.

Dionysius and the Theory of Italian Origins

Most later Greek and Roman scholars and writers agreed with Herodotus and perpetuated the tradition that the Etruscans had emigrated from Asia Minor to Italy. Over time, some incorporated the Pelasgians into this scenario. According to the classical Greeks, the Pelasgians were the original inhabitants of Greece and other lands bordering the Aegean Sea before the Greeks themselves entered the region. Supposedly, isolated pockets of Pelasgians survived into later times. And some writers claimed that the Etruscans were Pelasgians from Asia Minor or elsewhere who migrated to Italy.

However, a few ancient scholars disagreed. The most prominent among them was the Greek historian Dionysius, who, like Herodotus, came from Halicarnassus. In the first century B.C., Dionysius wrote a long history of Rome—*The Roman Antiquities*

—large portions of which survive. According to Dionysius, who was a more critical historian than Herodotus (who often simply repeated what he heard):

I am convinced that the Pelasgians were a different people from the Tyrrhenians. And I do not believe that the Tyrrhenians were Lydian settlers, as they do not speak the same language as the Lydians. Those are therefore probably closer to the truth who state that the Etruscan nation did not originate elsewhere, but was indigenous to the country [i.e., to northern Italy].[8]

A few early modern scholars thought that Dionysius might have been on the right track, as indeed he was. But they were largely overshadowed by those who agreed with Herodotus. There was also a third theory, which suggested that the Etruscans migrated into Italy from central Europe by way of the Alpine passes. Noted Etruscologist Ellen Macnamara summarizes the evidence for this theory and then tells how it more logically supports the notion of native Italian Etruscan origins:

[The] hypothesis [of central European origins] principally rests upon similarities noted between the cultures of central Europe and the people . . . [living] in Italy during the early first millennium B.C., and the evidence of inscriptions in Etruscan found in the valleys of the Alps. The former, however, may be best explained by trade, not migration, and the latter by the presence of Etruscan groups who fled into the mountains when the Gauls

PELASGIANS ON LEMNOS?

Among the ancient theories for the origins of the Etruscans was one that claimed they came from the Aegean island of Lemnos. Another associated them with the Pelasgians, a general name for the earliest inhabitants of Greece. In fact, a few Pelasgians were reported to have survived on Lemnos in later centuries, until expelled by the Athenians. The fifth-century B.C. historian Herodotus acknowledges this in his *Histories*.

> When the Pelasgians had been settled for some time in Lemnos . . . the crops [on the island] failed, the birth rate declined, and the cattle no longer increased as rapidly as before, so that the islanders began to suffer severely from lack of food and dwindling population. In these circumstances they sent to Delphi [home of the famous oracle] to ask advice on the best way of escaping from their troubles, and were told by the priestess to submit to whatever punishment the Athenians might choose to impose on them [in retaliation for offenses committed earlier against Athens]. . . . [No punishment occurred at this time.] But many years later [the Athenian general Miltiades] sailed . . . to Lemnos. On his arrival, he ordered the Pelasgians out of the island . . . and the [Pelasgians] obeyed.

[a Celtic people from beyond the Alps] overran [the northern reaches of Italy in the fifth century B.C.].[9]

Indeed, there is no convincing proof that the Etruscans came from anywhere outside of their traditional homeland of Etruria. "The overwhelming evidence of the archaeological record," scholars Barker and Rasmussen assert, "is that the origins of Etruscan society lie fundamentally in the later prehistoric communities of Etruria."[10]

Etruria in the Stone Age

Having established with reasonable certainty that the Etruscans originated in north-

ern Italy, scholars have ascertained the "where" of the origins of that ancient people. Just as important is the "when" and the "how." In other words, when did the inhabitants of Etruria first start living in organized communities? And how did these earliest Etruscans make a living, house themselves, and impact their environment?

By examining remnants of Italy's earliest societies, archaeologists have attempted to answer these questions. There is no way to tell exactly when the people who dwelled in scattered communities across prehistoric Etruria recognized themselves as a single culture, that neighboring peoples came to call Etruscan. Perhaps language was the first and strongest cultural factor that linked these early Etrurian communities. The Etruscan language was very different from Latin, Greek, and the other Indo-European tongues, which came to dominate the Mediterranean world in the early first millennium B.C. Scholars do not yet know where the Etruscan language came from and when it was first spoken in Etruria. But they think that an early form of it was in place there by 1000 B.C. and perhaps well before.

On the other hand, archaeologists can tell with reasonable certainty when the residents of Etruria began living in organized communities. The region was inhabited at least as early as 200,000 years ago, during the Stone Age (when tools and weapons were fashioned from stone). But for a long time the people were nomadic and made their livings by hunting and gathering. In approximately 5000 B.C. (about seven thousand years ago), the Etrurians adopted agriculture and settled down in permanent villages. They grew mostly cereal grains and raised sheep, goats, and pigs.

One reason that these farming communities thrived and grew larger and more numerous over time was the exceptionally favorable terrain and climate of Etruria. The soil was rich and the forests abundant, with a wide variety of plants and trees (notably beech, oak, chestnut, and pine). At the same time, springs and summers were long and warm and the winters short, mild, and moderately wet,

A farmer guides a plow drawn by oxen in this fifth-century B.C. bronze work found near the Etruscan city of Arretium.

making drought and famine rare and ensuring the prosperity of village life.

As for the physical appearance of these communities, at first most were small, with only a few families in residence. Archaeological studies show that the one- or two-room huts were made of branches, reeds, straw, and mud. Spaced around the perimeter of the huts were small gardens where the crops were grown (large fields were rare because the area was then heavily forested). The dead (or at least some members of the community) were buried in nearby caves. In the Grotta Patrizi, a cave in the mountains northwest of Rome, excavators found the remains of several Stone Age Etrurian villagers. The grave goods accompanying the bodies included stone knives, ceramic pots, and primitive jewelry.

The Advent of the Bronze Age

Eventually, the natives of Etruria began using metal tools and weapons, bringing the Stone Age to a close. From this point on, modern scholars date Etruria and Etruscan civilization by dividing its many centuries of existence into set ages or periods. For the sake of clarity and convenience, the names of these time blocks are the same as some of those employed for Greek civilization (i.e., Bronze Age, Iron Age, Orientalizing Period, Archaic Age, Classical Age, and Hellenistic Age). However, this does not mean that the dates of the Etruscan ages exactly

This model shows the likely appearance of an early Etruscan hut. The walls were made of branches packed with dried mud and clay.

match those of the Greek ones. For instance, the Archaic Age of Greece lasted from roughly 800 to 500 B.C., whereas the Etruscan Archaic Age is dated from circa 600 to circa 480 B.C.

The first metal exploited by the early Etrurians was copper, which was widespread in the region. They soon learned to mix the copper with a considerably rarer metal, tin, to make bronze, which is harder and more durable than plain copper. Scholars date the Italian Bronze Age from approximately 2000 to 900 B.C. During this period, the Etrurian settlements grew in size and their numbers increased manifold, signs of the added prosperity produced by metal tools and weapons. The villagers also expanded into the hills and mountains of Etruria, probably to exploit newly discovered deposits of copper and tin.

As might be expected, bronze weapons and tools were difficult and expensive to make, which made them very valuable. People found that they could be bartered and traded in exchange for other valuable goods. And possession of them, especially in large quantities, made a person wealthy, respected, and special—what archaeologists often call an "elite" in a community. Thus, the production and ownership of valuable metals stimulated the emergence of a new kind of leader. Before, a village chief might have been the strongest person or the best hunter or fighter. Now, he was the richest and most influential person, and, when possible, he passed his power on to his sons, who inherited it simply by birthright. As one expert puts it, the combination of increased economic activity, expansion of communities and their populations, and the emergence of wealthy elites

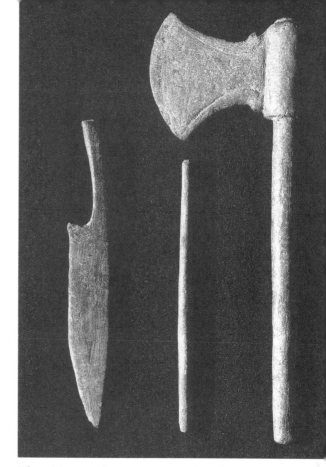

These Etruscan bronze weapons, found not far from Rome, date to the sixth century B.C.

signaled "the development of the chiefdom societies from which the Etruscan state societies swiftly developed."[11]

The Villanovans

The term *state society* refers to a society in which the people see themselves as a coherent, national unit with established territories and a central government that makes and enforces the local laws. All through the late Italian Bronze Age, the larger communities of Etruria were absorbing or gaining control of the smaller villages surrounding them and forming rudimentary political states. This process gained further steam beginning in about 900 B.C., which modern scholars mark as the start of the Iron Age in

Italy. It is also referred to as the Villanovan period. This name comes from the modern village of Villanova (near the city of Bologna), where in 1853 archaeologists first found remnants of the Iron Age culture.

At first, scholars suspected that the so-called Villanovans were outsiders who migrated into Etruria from beyond the Alps, bringing with them iron tools and weapons. Part of the reason why they seemed so different from the Bronze Age inhabitants was their burial customs. Instead of burying people in the ground (a practice called inhumation), the Villanovans primarily cremated their dead. However, later excavations showed that there was no discernible break in continuity between the Bronze and Iron Age Etrurian communities. The Villanovans were simply Etrurians who had begun to use iron along with bronze and had developed new burial customs.

Similarly, back when scholars thought the Etruscans had migrated into northern Italy, it was assumed that the Villanovans and Etruscans were two separate peoples. But it is now clear that the Villanovans *were* the Etruscans. "The fundamental cultural continuity between the ninth, eighth, and seventh centuries [B.C.] in Etruria," Macnamara points out, "makes it certain that the early Iron Age people were the true precursors of Etruscan civilization and that the inhabitants of Etruria during the Villanovan period were proto-Etruscans."[12]

These Villanovans, or early Etruscans, still lived largely in villages. However, by now some were full-fledged towns, which were most often built on highly defensible hilltops that allowed easy command and control of neighboring valleys. Studies of cemeteries and pottery of the period in-

dicate that about ten or twelve major towns came to dominate most of Etruria. The five largest (Caere, Tarquinii, Veii, Volsinii, and Vulci) would later become leading Etruscan cities.

What did the dwellings in these towns look like? A fairly clear picture comes from pottery urns (for storing the ashes of the dead) modeled to look like houses, which have been found in Villanovan cemeteries. They indicate that houses in Iron Age Tarquinii and Vulci were both rectangular and oval in shape, the latter having conical roofs. As in earlier times, the walls were made mostly of thatch and dried mud. But now the mass of interwoven branches, reeds, and clay was often strengthened by vertical and horizontal pieces of timber and/or laid on a stone foundation. Many of these houses also had small porches extending outward from and protecting their single doors. Wooden posts held up the roofs of the porches.

Inside the Villanovan houses, the floors were probably mainly dirt. However, there is some evidence of stone floors. And excavators have found some houses with shallow basements dug beneath the stones in which to store food or perhaps valuables. The center of a typical house had a stone hearth for heating and cooking. The smoke from the hearth exited through a hole in the roof. The largest towns of this period had several hundred such houses and populations in the hundreds or low thousands.

These towns were still separate social and political entities and did not coalesce into a central state or nation. In fact, such widespread centralization never occurred in Etruria, even later when Etruscan civilization was at its height. Like the city-states of ancient Greece,

URNS SHAPED LIKE HOUSES

The best archaeological evidence for how early Etruscan houses looked takes the form of hut-urns, as explained by noted scholar Nigel Spivey in his book about Etruscan art.

As a concept, the hut-urn is not unique to Etruria. But if any single artifact could be said to embody the predominant surviving [form] of Etruscan art and architecture generally, then the hut-urn would be a strong candidate. It is patently a miniature [version] of the sort of dwelling actually in use at the time, with its oval or circular form, and its ridged and gabled sloping roof with smoke openings and closable door. . . . Windows may be suggested [on an urn] by exterior decoration. . . . Inside the hut would be placed the cremated remains of the deceased. The process of cremation does not normally reduce the entire body to ashes, and in some cases the bone remains within a hut-urn are [substantial].

This Etruscan hut-urn was made sometime between 900 and 600 B.C.

the major urban centers of Etruria always remained fiercely independent and saw themselves as tiny separate nations.

Phoenician and Greek Influences

So far, the independent Villanovan, or early Etruscan, towns have been examined in the context of their immediate surroundings, the countryside of Etruria. Yet they did not exist in a vacuum, cut off from other Mediterranean peoples. To the contrary, Etruria's pleasant climate, its rich soil, and especially its abundant supplies of metal ores attracted the attention of a number of outside groups.

Probably the first of these were the Phoenicians, a prosperous maritime people based along the coasts of Palestine, in the eastern Mediterranean. In the late 800s B.C., the Phoenicians founded the city of Carthage, in North Africa, and went on to establish trading posts in Spain, southern Gaul (what is now France), and the islands of Sardinia and Sicily. The latter excursions brought them into close proximity with the western Italian coasts, including those of Etruria. Eventually a vigorous trade ensued in which the early Etruscans received Spanish gold and other valuables in exchange for their own copper and tin. The Phoenicians also set up small trading posts at Etruscan ports, including Punicum, the port town of Tarquinii, and Pyrgi, the port of Caere.

Phoenician sailors and merchants prepare for a voyage in this nineteenth-century woodcut. The Etruscans conducted a vigorous trade with the Phoenicians.

Not surprisingly, the influx of Phoenician trade goods—including wine, olive oil, textiles, glasswork, and much more—as well as foreign customs and artistic and religious ideas, steadily transformed Etruria. Noted historian Michael Grant writes:

The Phoenicians, at the center of a huge cultural melting pot, obtained their aesthetic [artistic and social] ideas from a great number of different sources and were tireless pickers-up of the customs, methods, and arts of surrounding lands. . . . [So through Phoenician traders] various Syrian, Cypriot, Egyptian, [and] Mesopotamian influences were already reaching Etruria in the second half of the eighth century B.C. and became more numerous still around 700 B.C. . . . The Phoenicians . . . owing to their desire for Etruscan metals, fulfilled a decisive role in the transmission of the Near Eastern elements that subsequently played such a vital part in the development of Etruria.[13]

The Greeks followed on the heels of the Phoenicians and had an even more profound influence on developing Etruscan culture. The first Greek trading post in Italy was established about 760 B.C. on the coastal island of Ischia, which the Greeks called Pithecusae (or Pithekoussai). In the six or seven decades that followed, dozens of other Greek settlements sprang up on the coasts of southern Italy and the nearby island of Sicily.

The influence of the Greeks on the people of Etruria in these years can be seen from a massive influx of Greek pottery in the region. (Archaeologists know when and where the Greek pottery they find in Etruria was made because they can match it with known types and styles from Greece.) Some Greeks actually worked in Etruscan towns and probably passed on knowledge of the potter's wheel and other artistic techniques. The natives of Etruria also adopted Greek clothing styles, fabric designs, and artistic motifs, which began to adorn the walls of Etruscan tombs.

Evidence excavated from these tombs indicates that the massive inflow of goods, especially luxury goods, and ideas from Greek sources affected early Etruscan society in numerous ways. At this stage, the most far-reaching was in the social realm. Whatever social divisions had existed in the Bronze Age and early Iron Age were now heightened. A few people in each town became increasingly rich and powerful and exerted more authority over the lower classes. At the same time, these classes further divided into groups of people who specialized in one area or another. New kinds of artisans and merchants joined the already existing farmers, miners, metalsmiths, and traders.

These changes in the local societies of Etruria were rapid and extensive. Yet they marked only the beginning of the transformation of the region under the influence of the Greeks. Soon, the Greeks would introduce even more profound ideas, including military ones, that would help facilitate the rise of powerful Etruscan city-states. Italy's first truly great native civilization was about to emerge.

CHAPTER TWO

THE RAPID RISE OF THE ETRUSCAN CITY-STATES

Toward the end of the Iron Age (or Villanovan period), the Etruscans had been suddenly exposed to outside cultural influences, principally from the eastern Mediterranean region. First the Phoenicians and then the Greeks had developed prosperous trade relations and cultural links with Etruscan towns, especially those lying near the sea. Beginning in about 700 B.C., these eastern influences, in particular those from Greece, substantially increased in number, diversity, and effect. They became so strong, in fact, that they significantly transformed Etruscan civilization in a relatively short time span. For this reason, scholars call the roughly century-long era that started in 700 B.C. the Etruscans' Orientalizing Period. (The name comes from the now quaint use of the term *Orient* to describe the lands of the eastern Mediterranean and Near East.)

In the Orientalizing Period, Etruscan culture took on the form that the early Greco-Roman writers knew and described. That form consisted of a group of populous and powerful city-states that rapidly rose in Etruria and began to spread their influence across large portions of Italy. Meanwhile, thanks to an ever-increasing volume of foreign trade, the Etruscans were becoming major players in a much larger sphere. As Barker and Rasmussen explain:

> Whereas the earlier archaeology of Etruria can in large part be explained without recourse to moving beyond the confines of central Italy, Etruscan culture emerges now, after 700 B.C., as one of the leading lights on the Mediterranean stage and, with its international contacts, can only be properly discussed in the context of the wider Mediterranean setting.[14]

That wider setting for Etruscan culture was shaped most significantly by the Greeks, as in this period wave after wave of them migrated to Italy and established new settlements. The evidence indicates that the Etruscans were very impressed with Greek arts and culture. So Etruscan civilization did more than simply expand its wealth, population, and territory as a result of the increased volume of trade. Its society and culture also grew richer thanks to the inflow of new artistic and technical knowledge, as well as literacy (after borrowing an alphabet from the Greeks).

Tombs Reveal Increased Prosperity

For modern archaeologists, these cultural advances are plainly revealed and reflected in the Etruscan tombs of the period, which became much more numerous and richly decorated than ever before. The cemeteries, which had existed on the outskirts of the towns for centuries, now expanded greatly in size. (However, it took several more centuries for the largest ones excavated thus far to reach their present size.) The biggest of these tombs are impressive enough to be called true architectural works, and in fact, scholars view them as Italy's first examples of monumental (large-scale) stone architecture.

Typically, such a tomb consisted of one or more chambers carved out of *tufo*, the soft, very ancient volcanic stone found in large quantities across Etruria. Above the roof of the tomb, the builders piled up a mound of earth called a tumulus. Inside, there were rock-cut couches or shelves on which to place the bodies of the deceased.

This cutaway drawing reconstructs the connected chambers of an Etruscan tomb. Typically, these rooms were buried beneath a mound of earth.

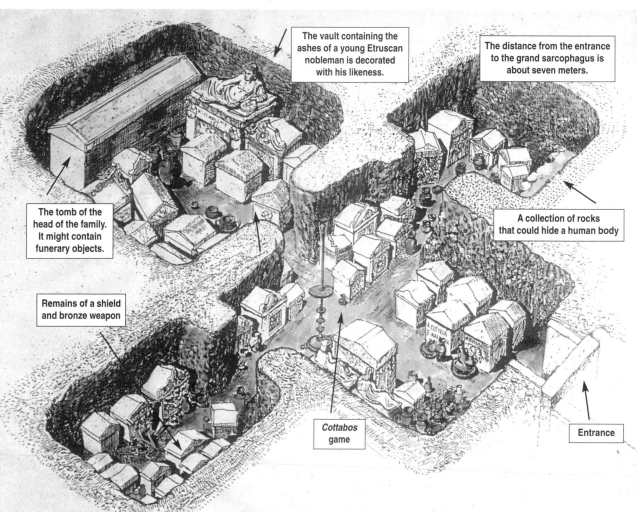

The vault containing the ashes of a young Etruscan nobleman is decorated with his likeness.

The distance from the entrance to the grand sarcophagus is about seven meters.

The tomb of the head of the family. It might contain funerary objects.

A collection of rocks that could hide a human body

Remains of a shield and bronze weapon

Cottabos game

Entrance

Sometimes, however, urns bearing people's ashes were placed on these shelves, for Etruscan burial practices in this period were a mixture of inhumation and cremation. Most of those cremated appear to have been wealthy aristocrats, suggesting that cremation was a mark of high status.

In fact, wealth and status seem to have played a crucial role in Etruscan funerary practices. The larger the tomb, the more and better the grave goods that were piled inside, often including expensive pottery, metal sculptures, and gold and silver jewelry. The largest of all these monuments have come to be called *tombe principesche*, Italian for "princely tombs." The name is well chosen, since having a big, opulent funeral was surely a way for the rich and powerful to show off their and their families' prestige and power. "In a sense, funerals are theater and display," Barker and Rasmussen point out.

> Quite apart from the elaborate rituals acted out and the expensive grave goods carried in procession, they provide an unequalled opportunity for the ruling class to reinforce its superior position in society and to maintain it by means of a permanent architectural monument for posterity [future generations] to wonder at.[15]

For these reasons, an Etruscan tomb and its contents (at least those items that have

The splendor of many Etruscan tombs is exemplified by the Tomb of the Leopards (named for the leopards depicted above the human figures).

This ivory comb from an Etruscan tomb is on display in a museum in Florence. Grooming items are common in Etruscan tombs.

survived the looters) tell scholars a great deal about the state of society at the moment when they were deposited in the ground. First, the number and quality of the grave goods indicate the level of wealth and luxury enjoyed by the upper classes. The kinds and diversity of the goods show the breadth of foreign trade and who that trade was with. For example, large numbers of vases and other pots from specific places in Greece and the Near East have been found in these tombs. Tableware, utensils, mirrors, and combs placed inside, ostensibly for the dead to use in the afterlife, reveal what people used for eating and grooming. And sculptures and paintings adorning the tomb show clothing and hairstyles and various social activities and customs.

Population Increases and Urbanization

There is a limit, however, to what can be learned from studying Etruscan tombs. After all, people did not actually live in them. Also, an undetermined proportion of the grave goods and art in such tombs was ceremonial in nature and death-related and may not reflect the average or common customs and practices of the living. Thus, scholars must be careful not to jump to what may be the wrong conclusions in trying to reconstruct Etruscan society solely from studies of tombs.

Much more might be learned about Etruscan society from examining the remains of the major cities. Because most of them lie beneath the structures of later cities, large-scale excavations of these sites have not

Workmen raise artifacts from an underground tomb. Each Etruscan town had one or more cemeteries outside its urban center.

been feasible to date. Still, archaeologists do know where these cities are located and in some places have excavated isolated buildings and streets. There are also numerous mentions of these cities in ancient sources. Combining this evidence with that gathered in excavations in the countryside, scholars have been able to piece together a reasonably clear picture of the identities and territories of the leading cities of Etruria in this era. They may be more accurately termed *city-states*, since each consisted of a central town (what archaeologists call an urban center) surrounded by a network of dependent villages and farms. Together, the urban center, villages, and farms made up what was in effect a tiny country.

The ancient sources consistently mention twelve major Etruscan cities. This makes sense because it roughly corresponds to the number of major Villanovan towns, from which the cities obviously grew. And archaeologists have identified twelve to fifteen major Etruscan urban centers that dominated the scene in the Orientalizing Period and the two centuries that followed it.

These cities grew at the expense of several of the smaller towns and villages that surrounded them, since over time people from the countryside migrated into the urban centers. As in similar situations in other ages and places, they were likely attracted by better economic opportunities and the enhanced security of the cities' defensive walls. Speaking of defense, these cities were all located on hilltops or other highly defensive positions. Another factor that determined whether a town would grow into a major city was its proximity to rich sources of metal ores and to trade routes with the Greeks. If all of these factors were favorable, the town's population rose rapidly in this era. Modern estimates for the populations of the major Etruscan cities by the end of the Orientalizing Period range from eight thousand to thirty-five thousand people each.

Multiplying an average of twenty thousand people times twelve to fifteen cities gives a total of more than a quarter of a million people. That sounds like —and indeed is—a substantial number for a region the size of Etruria in that era, yet it represents only part of the larger population picture. Although some of the rural settlements were abandoned as the cities grew, many other rural settlements prospered and new ones appeared. The result was a population explosion in the countryside that occurred at the same time that the cities were growing in size. This means that a city-state with an urban center having twenty thousand inhabitants likely encompassed and controlled a region with a total population of three, four, or five times that number.

How do archaeologists determine such increases (or decreases) in population in a given ancient region? To do so, they must estimate the number and density of local population centers in that region. One of the principal methods used is called field walking. Groups of investigators (often students apprenticing with an archaeological team) walk back and forth across farmers' fields, usually in the autumn, after plowing. Invariably, the plowing digs up and

This Etruscan city gate has survived and is still in use in the town of Todi.

exposes small pieces of ancient pottery. More often than not, these fragments approximately mark the sites of ancient farmsteads and villages, where people once accumulated many pottery storage vessels. (In most cases, the houses and barns, made of wood and other perishable materials, have long since disintegrated, but some of the sturdy fired pots have survived.) One field walking survey conducted in the region of Veii, in southern Etruria, revealed 137 farms and villages in the Orientalizing Period, compared with only 16 in the Villanovan era in the same region. This clearly indicates a substantial increase in population in a relatively brief time span.

The Major Etruscan Cities

Experts not only have determined Etruria underwent large-scale population increases beginning about 700 B.C. but have identified the major urban centers that grew in the region. The southernmost city of Etruria was Caere (modern Cerveteri), located near the coast about twenty-two miles northwest of Rome. It was erected atop a low hill with rocky cliffs at the base and surrounded by a stout defensive wall. The city's cemeteries were situated at the bottom of the cliffs and on nearby hills. A well-maintained road ran about four miles to Caere's port of Pyrgi, where two temples and other buildings have been excavated.

A mere fifteen miles east of Caere and just twelve miles north of Rome lay another important Etruscan city-state, Veii. The city of Veii was dominated by an acropolis (a Greek word meaning "the city's high place"), a central hill partially bordered by cliffs. The inhabitants erected high stone walls to protect the parts of the town that

lay beyond the safety of the cliffs. Veii was the closest Etruscan city to Rome, so economic and cultural contacts and disputes between the two were likely frequent in the Orientalizing Period.

The rest of the major Etruscan cities were situated farther to the north. Considering those near the coast first, about twenty miles northwest of Caere lay the prosperous and powerful city of Tarquinii, located about three miles inland from the sea on the Marta River. Its extensive territory seems to have extended northeastward for at least twenty miles to Lake Bolsena. On the banks of the Fiora River, a few miles north of Tarquinii, lay the city of Vulci, both then and now known for its many and unusually rich surrounding tombs. Traveling some thirty-five miles northwest of Vulci one came to Rusellae (modern Roselle), and going in the same direction another twelve miles one arrived at Vetulonia. Moving still farther northward brought a traveler to Populonia, the only large Etruscan city situated directly on the seacoast. Populonia's surrounding territory was known for its particularly rich deposits of metal-bearing rocks.

For a tour of the inland Etruscan cities, one could start at Veii in the south and go northward about fifty miles to Volsinii (modern Orvieto), set atop an imposing, cliff-lined rocky outcrop. Twenty miles north of Volsinii, on the Chiana River, lay Clusium (modern Chiusi). Clusium was a very large city-state that bordered the territories of Volsinii in the south and Rusellae in the west. Located in the hills north and east of Clusium were three more Etruscan city-states: Perusia, Cortona, and Arretium (modern Arezzo). And northwest of these cities lay two more, Volterrae and Faesulae

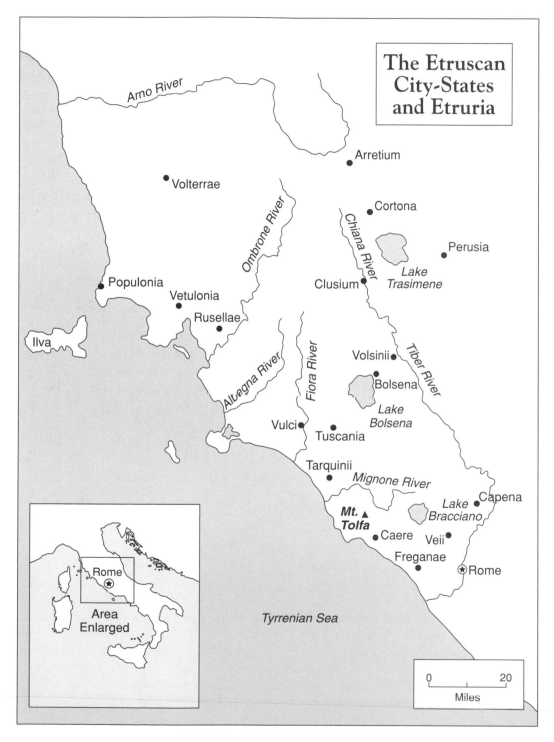

The Etruscan City-States and Etruria

Arno River

Arretium

Volterrae

Ombrone River

Cortona

Perusia

Chiana River

Lake Trasimene

Populonia

Vetulonia

Clusium

Rusellae

Ilva

Allegna River

Fiora River

Volsinii

Tiber River

Bolsena

Lake Bolsena

Vulci

Tuscania

Tarquinii

Mignone River

Mt. Tolfa

Lake Bracciano

Capena

Caere

Veii

Freganae

Rome

Rome

Area Enlarged

Tyrrenian Sea

0   20
Miles

(near modern Florence). The following brief description of Volterrae by Ellen Macnamara could well apply in most of its details to many of the other Etruscan urban centers:

> The metropolis was set upon a lofty summit, visible over a wide area and surrounded by a formidable . . . [defensive] wall . . . built of large, squared blocks set in courses. . . . The urban area has been continuously occupied through Roman to modern times. . . . Outside the city, chamber tombs of great families are known, usually rough hewn from the rock. . . . The few scattered Etruscan tombs known within the territory of Volterrae suggest widespread farming settlements [encircling the urban center].[16]

Eastern Trade Goods and Artistic Influences

As has been pointed out by many experts, among the major reasons that these cities rapidly grew large and prosperous in the Orientalizing Period were trade and cultural advances. And the Greeks were heavily involved in both of these areas. Greek merchant ships loaded with goods of all kinds docked at Etruscan ports, and Greek merchants traveled from Italian Greek cities overland into Etruria. The Greeks introduced pottery containers of every conceivable shape, along with many other products from the Greek city-states situated around the Aegean Sea.

Yet the trade goods entering Etruria were not limited to Greek-made products. The Greeks themselves had recently been strongly influenced by Near Eastern artistic styles and motifs. (Scholars date the Orien-

talizing Period of Greek pottery and art to about 720 to 600 B.C.) And they copied eastern styles and imported eastern goods. Not surprisingly, therefore, Greek traders brought goods from several other eastern lands into Italy. These included many luxury items, such as large, finely decorated seashells from the Indian Ocean and Red Sea; carved and painted beads and trinkets from Egypt; carved ivory from Syria; ostrich eggs from Mesopotamia; and silver vessels from Cyprus and Phoenicia (also brought to Italy by the Phoenicians themselves).

Well-to-do Etruscans enjoyed collecting and showing off such finery, which strengthened their social and perhaps political superiority over the common people. At the same time, the inflow of exotic goods and foreign ideas stimulated Etruscan artisans to produce more and better luxury items of their own. Some were what would today be called knockoffs, produced by local cottage industries that made copies of the most popular Greek items. Pottery from Corinth, in southern Greece, for example, was particularly prized and imitated by local Etruscan potters. On the other hand, some locally made products were more original and very finely crafted, especially gold cups, bowls, and brooches and other types of jewelry.

Greek Cultural Influences

The Greeks and Etruscans did more than trade and exchange ideas, however. Some Greeks actually moved to Etruscan cities and established themselves as artisans, bought property, and married Etruscans. Evidence from tombs at Ischia, the important Greek trading post on Italy's western coast, suggests that some Greek traders (who were all males) took Etruscan wives. Where the husbands

The Remains of Ancient Tarquinii

In this excerpt from his book about the Etruscans, noted scholar Michael Grant discusses the rise of Tarquinii and some of the artifacts that have survived from that important Etruscan city-state.

The first Etruscan center to respond to an external desire for its metals by completing the process of urbanization . . . [was] Tarquinii, on its defensible height beside the Marta River. . . . Early Etruscan cities generally display a blend of old and new. While retaining cultural features going back to their own pre-urban past, they produce an outburst of novel developments arising out of their newly acquired wealth. Tarquinii is no exception. There is continuity with the local past in the unbroken series of artifacts found in its cemeteries, but at the same time the impact of the novel Greek commerce is vigorously felt. . . . Like the other cities of Etruria, Tarquinii, as far as the dwellings of the living are concerned, has virtually disappeared. . . . Yet not everything has gone. We can see from the walls that the place had a circumference of five miles. . . . Inside those walls . . . magnetic surveys comprising tens of thousands of computer-processed measurements have revealed the general plan the city eventually assumed, the design of its principal streets, and sometimes even the outlines of single buildings.

and wives were buried together, the women's jewelry and other grave goods are identical to those in Etruscan tombs of the period.

There is also the famous story of Lucumo, told by the great first-century B.C. Roman historian Livy. In this tale, Lucumo is the product of a mixed Greek and Etruscan marriage. According to Livy, Demaratus, a Greek from Corinth, emigrated to Italy, settled in Tarquinii, and there married an Etruscan woman. They had two sons, one of whom they named Lucumo. When he grew into manhood, Lucumo married Tanaquil, a young woman from an aristocratic Etruscan

family, and the combination of their considerable inheritances made them very wealthy. Lucumo could not assume a leadership position in the community, however, because he was not a full-blooded Etruscan.

For this reason, the young couple decided to leave Tarquinii and settle in Rome, which at the time was, in Livy's words, "a young and rising community." Livy continues:

There would be opportunities [in Rome] for an active and courageous man in a place where all advancement came swiftly and depended upon ability. . . . The pair had reached Janiculum [a hill across the Tiber River from Rome] and were sitting together in their carriage, when an eagle dropped gently down and snatched off the cap which Lucumo was wearing. Up went the bird with a great clangor of wings until, a minute later, it swooped down again and, as if it had been sent by heaven for that very purpose, neatly replaced the cap on Lucumo's head, and then vanished into the blue. Tanaquil, like most Etruscans, was well skilled in [interpreting divine signs], and joyfully accepted the omen. Flinging her arms around her husband's neck, she told him . . . "Consider from what quarter of the sky the eagle came, what god sent it as his messenger! Did it not declare its message by coming to your *head* — the highest part of you? Did it not take the crown, as it were, from a human head, only to restore it by heaven's approval, where it belongs?"[17]

Thus, Tanaquil's interpretation of the incident with the eagle was that it foreshadowed her husband becoming an important leader in Rome. As Livy told it, she was right. Lucumo took the name of Lucius Tarquinius Priscus and in time rose to become

A MIXED MARRIAGE PRODUCES A FAMOUS SON

In his *History of Rome from Its Foundation*, the Roman historian Livy told about the origins of Rome's fifth king, Lucius Tarquinius Priscus, who began as Lucumo, the son of a Greek father and Etruscan mother.

In the course of the reign [of Rome's fourth king] a man named Lucumo left Tarquinii, where he was born, and came to settle in Rome. He was ambitious and wealthy and hoped to rise to a position of eminence there, such as his native town was never likely to afford him. For, though born at Tarquinii, he was by blood an alien, being the son of Demaratus of Corinth. Demaratus had been forced by political troubles to leave his country, and happened to settle in Tarquinii, where he married and had two sons, Lucumo and Arruns. [Arruns died young, but] Lucumo survived his father and inherited all his property. . . . [Lucumo] became in time as proud as he was wealthy, and his self-confidence was further increased by his marriage to Tanaquil, an aristocratic young woman who was not of a sort to put up with humbler circumstances in her married life than those she had previously been accustomed to.

Among the many Greek influences on the Etruscans were myths. These Etruscan painted plaques depict the Greek myth known as the Judgment of Paris.

Rome's fifth king. (Unlike Tarquinii, Rome already had a tradition of allowing foreign-born men to rule.)

The story of Lucumo's rise to the Roman kingship is likely a mixture of fable and truth. The parts involving omens and fate were obviously added later. As in other ancient tales about kings and queens, they justified their rule by showing that the gods supposedly approved of it. On the other hand, the idea of a Greek marrying an Etruscan and achieving success in a neighboring Italian city is perfectly consistent with the cultural exchanges and mixed marriages reflected in the archaeological record.

Bilingual Generations and the Alphabet

In fact, a number of clues revealed by excavators suggest that mixed Greek and Etruscan marriages may have been a key element in one of the most important of all cultural exchanges. Scholars have known for some time

that the Etruscans first began writing down their language at about the beginning of the Orientalizing Period (or, based on the most recent evidence, perhaps slightly earlier). These early writings took the form of brief inscriptions on pots and tomb walls. And they utilized the alphabet that the Greeks had recently borrowed from the Phoenicians. (The Greeks had altered it somewhat to fit their own tongue, mainly by adding vowels; the original Phoenician version had only consonants.)

Close studies of early Greek and Etruscan inscriptions have led most archaeologists to suspect that the Greeks at Ischia (and maybe the nearby town of Cumae) taught their alphabet to the Etruscans with whom they traded there. Moreover, the evidence of mixed marriages in Ischia strengthens this supposition. It helps to explain "how the Etruscans began to use Greek alphabetic writing so suddenly," Barker and Rasmussen point out, specifically the alphabet of Ischia/ Cumae, for the intricacies of a writing system are unlikely to be learned simply through casual trading encounters. But intermarriage entails a second generation at least partly bilingual, and its members would have been in the best position to promote the new script. Able to mix freely among both ethnic groups, they may also have been among the first to prosper from the international trading opportunities opened by the arrival of the Greeks in the first place. The Artiaco Tomb at Cumae [in which it appears that an Etruscan was buried with full honors in a Greek town] may then be the resting place not of a [full-blooded] Etruscan, but of a half-Greek, half-Etruscan of the second generation.[18]

The remarkably rapid rise of the major Etruscan city-states in the late 700s and throughout the 600s B.C. was therefore attributable to a series of factors mainly connected to Greek contacts. An influx of Greek products, artistic ideas, and other cultural elements stimulated the production of local wealth. This, in turn, strengthened the position of old aristocratic Etruscan families and led to more pronounced class divisions. At the same time, economic opportunities opened up for enterprising individuals of the middle and upper classes, which contributed to large population increases and movements of families from villages to cities or from one city to another. Finally, Greek cultural influences were further facilitated and cemented by intermarriages between Greeks and Etruscans. And among these influences, the Etruscan adoption of the Greek alphabet was one of the most important.

One must not discount the contributions made by the Etruscans themselves in all of these events. However, it is clear that, without the Greeks, the Etruscans' rise to prominence in Mediterranean affairs may not have occurred, or at least would have happened in a different way.

CHAPTER THREE

THE ETRUSCANS AT THE HEIGHT OF THEIR POWER

In ancient Etruria, the Orientalizing Period was followed by the Archaic Age, which lasted roughly from 600 to 480 B.C. It was in the Archaic Age that the Etruscans reached their height of power and prosperity as a people. The major city-states were bustling with activity, ranging from farming and local industries to foreign trade and colonization. Regarding the latter, groups of Etruscans migrated both southward and northward, perhaps driven by population pressures in their homelands as well as by the lure of economic opportunities elsewhere.

By the end of the age, Etruscans had taken over a number of ancient Italian towns outside of Etruria and established several new ones. Meanwhile, individual Etruscans migrated to neighboring Italian cities, including Rome, and rose to leadership positions there. For a while, it may have seemed to many non-Etruscans that the whole Italian peninsula would eventually become "Etruscanized" in one way or another.

Prosperity gained from trade, both local and foreign, was one factor that made this expansion possible. Another crucial factor was military in nature. One of the innovations that the Greeks passed on to the Etruscans during the Orientalizing Period was a series of military innovations, including better

armor and weapons. The Etruscans eagerly absorbed these ideas and in the Archaic Age used them to considerable advantage.

However, two major factors kept the Etruscans from achieving total domination of Italy at the moment when their potential was greatest. First, during their expansion they eventually came up against Greek and Roman armies, which were largely superior in organization and ability. Second, and perhaps more telling, the Etruscans never achieved the political unity that was essential to their ultimate success. The Etruscan city-states fought one another as often as—or maybe even more than—they fought non-Etruscans; this allowed the enemies who surrounded them to grow increasingly stronger.

Etruscan Disunity

The disunity that existed in Etruria in the Archaic Age was almost certainly deep-rooted. It appears to have been both internal—affecting the classes within each city-state—and external—pitting state against state. Because so little is known about Etruscan society and political developments, modern scholars can trace these divisions and struggles only with great difficulty. Occasional words and short passages in the works of later Greco-Roman writers offer some clues. The rest of the picture must be pieced together from surviving Etruscan wall paintings (mostly in tombs), short Etruscan inscriptions, and other scattered archaeological evidence.

The combined clues suggest that foreign influences and the influx of wealth into Etruria in the 700s and 600s B.C. brought much power to a select few in the Etruscan

A watercolor shows Etruscan soldiers in the 700s and early 600s B.C. Only the wealthy could afford a full array of armor and weapons.

cities. These aristocrats came to occupy the top of the social pyramid. And they were able to maintain their power partly by using their wealth and influence to provide for followers and supporters from the lower classes. This is not surprising, since similar social developments occurred in many Greek cities, as well as in Rome, in roughly the same period.

However, another development in Etruria, one also mirrored in Rome and numerous Greek cities, was discontent among many in the lower classes at not having a say in local affairs. In time, to avoid civil strife, the big landowning families had to concede some political rights to at least the most prominent members of the lower classes. In particular, men who could afford armor and weapons—the local soldiery —had to be appeased. Otherwise the aristocrats could not hold on to their power.

In Greece and Rome, such concessions most often took the form of popular assemblies in which landowners (who doubled as soldiers in times of emergency) could discuss policy and approve of the community's leaders. It is unclear whether this happened in the Etruscan cities, for no evidence of any sort of democratic trends in Etruria has yet been found. This may explain why struggles between the aristocrats and successful nonaristocrats continued. And it may be that the outcomes of these struggles were decided less by compromise and social change and more by confrontation and naked force. There is evidence to suggest that in the latter half of the Archaic Age military strongmen arose in some of the Etruscan states. (Lars Porsenna, of Clusium, who figured prominently in Rome's early history, was one.) Some of these leaders may have been nonaristocrats who had managed to gain the backing of most of the local soldiering class.

As for external Etruscan disunity in this era, the evidence seems to indicate that the city-states of Etruria rarely, if ever, united in any common cause. They did form a league with representatives that met on a regular basis at a more or less central spot near Lake Bolsena. But this was basically a religious organization designed to honor the gods that all Etruscans worshipped. It was not a political federation, as Grant explains:

> Their league was not an effective body. It remained, practically speaking, insignificant and inoperative as a political and military force. We have no knowledge of the league ever entering upon a treaty or alliance with an external power. . . . It failed conspicuously to produce unity or united action among the city-states of Etruria.[19]

Indeed, scholars have identified several examples of most of the Etruscan states refusing to come together to help one of their number that was in jeopardy. In most of its

Among the Etruscan military figures who rose to prominence during the Archaic Age was Lars Porsenna (on throne).

bloody wars against Rome, for instance, Veii received no aid from the other Etruscan cities. And this surely sealed its fate in the end. In addition, a number of wall paintings from Etruria clearly show Etruscans fighting other Etruscans.

Greek-Style Armor and Weapons

Despite their lack of unity, various Etruscan groups successfully expanded their interests at the expense of neighboring peoples during the Archaic Age. This was due partly to the industriousness and determination of these groups and their leaders. But it was also attributable in large part to the military innovations the Greeks introduced into Etruria. Before the infusion of Greek military ideas, Etruscan warriors were only lightly armored. Typically a soldier wore a thin metal cuirass (breastplate), either rectangular or round in shape, held in place by leather straps; now referred to as a "pectoral," in most cases it protected only the center of the chest, not the entire upper torso.

The early Etruscan warrior also wore a metal helmet shaped like an inverted bowl, topped by a tall, thin metal ridge that tapered up to a point. Modern scholars call this a Villanovan helmet because it was the most popular type in the Villanovan stage of Etruscan civilization. Another popular Italian-style helmet used by the Etruscans in the Archaic Age was the so-called Negau type, which was conical in shape and often topped by a crest made of horsehair. None of these helmets protected the face, which was a significant drawback.

With possible occasional exceptions, this was the extent of pre-Greek Etruscan armor. For further protection the warriors did have shields, which were round or oval and had a single handgrip in the back (which made holding one in a defensive position for longer than a

few minutes quite tiring). And they fought with bronze or iron spears, swords, axes, and daggers.

Such armor and weapons were very expensive, so only men of the upper classes could afford to own them (as shown by the fact that this gear appears only in wealthy tombs). Therefore, the core units of early Etruscan armies must have been made up of men from aristocratic families. They were likely supported by units of men from the lower classes who wore no armor and either

This helmet from the eighth century B.C. *features the pointed metal ridge that was characteristic of early Etruscan helmets.*

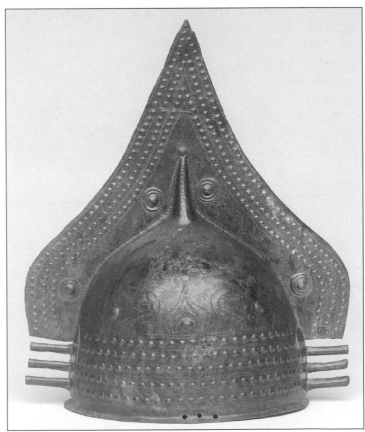

THE NEGAU HELMET

In this excerpt from his book *Greece and Rome at War*, noted scholar-illustrator Peter Connolly gives these details about the Negau helmet, which remained popular among Etruscan warriors even after their adoption of various Greek military items.

> The Negau type [of helmet was] named after a village in Yugoslavia [now Croatia and Bosnia] where a large number of them were found. . . . The earliest datable example comes from the Tomb of the Warrior at Vulci (ca. 525 B.C.). This type remained in use unchanged right down to the 4th and possibly the 3rd century [B.C.]. Attached to the inside of the rim of these helmets was a flat ring of bronze with stitching holes along the inside edge to hold the inner cap. This was necessary to keep the helmet well up on the head. This helmet type evolved from a group of sixth-century [B.C.] helmets referred to . . . under the general name of pot helmets.

A surviving example of the Negau helmet.

wielded second-rate swords and farm implements or threw rocks. In general, armies were probably small (a few hundred soldiers and on rare occasions a few thousand) and were raised and commanded more often by leading local families or clans than by the city-states themselves.

In the early Archaic Age, however, Greek innovations began to change this approach to warfare. The Greek military system was built around heavily armored infantry soldiers called hoplites. A typical hoplite wore a highly protective torso-covering cuirass made of bronze (or several layers of heavy linen). His helmet was often Chalcidian (northern Aegean) in style (though other styles were in use), featuring strips of metal that protected the cheeks, nose, and neck. The hoplite also wore greaves (lower-leg protectors) made of beaten bronze. His principal weapon was a six- or seven-foot-long thrusting spear, which he jabbed overhand at an enemy soldier. He also carried a short sword, usually of bronze but occasionally of iron, which he used if he lost or broke his spear.

A hoplite's most distinctive piece of gear was his round shield (*hoplon* or *aspis*), which was about three feet in diameter and had a gripping system far superior to that of early Italian shields. In the center of the inside of the shield was a bronze strip with a loop, through which the hoplite passed his left forearm; on the rim was a leather handle, which he grasped with his left hand. Because this system allowed the shield to rest on the hoplite's arm, it helped to relieve the burden of the shield's considerable weight. Also, if the need arose, the hoplite could let go of the handle and hold a spare weapon in his left hand without losing his shield.

By the early 500s B.C., the core, or first-class, units of Etruscan armies had largely adopted the armor and weapons of the Greek hoplites. However, the acquisition of such gear was still the responsibility of individuals (and perhaps families). So the change-over was neither quick nor universal. Some Etruscan fighters still used old-style pectorals and Negau helmets throughout the Archaic Age (in the case of the helmets, well beyond). And some warriors freely mixed old and new gear. A painting in one tomb at Caere, for example, shows a soldier wearing a Chalcidian helmet and an Etr-

uscan pectoral. And another tomb painting at Vulci shows a warrior with a Greek hoplite shield and a Negau helmet.

Lack of Battlefield Cohesion?

That the Etruscans adopted Greek armor and weapons is well attested by the evidence. Far less clear is the degree to which the Etruscans utilized the distinctive and highly effective battlefield formation and tactics of Greek hoplites. How did Etruscan commanders organize their hoplites and support troops in the field? And how did these soldiers fight?

First, one must consider how Greek hoplites fought. Usually they stood in ranks (lines), one behind the other, creating a formation called a phalanx. Although eight ranks was the most common depth of a phalanx, sometimes commanders called for more than eight or as few as three or four. In essence, the phalanx was a formidable wall of upright shields and forward-pointing spears. And when its members marched forward in unison, they were very difficult to stop or defend against.

Evidence shows that a few Italian peoples did adopt the phalanx and the battlefield tactics associated with it. In particular, the Romans did so during the Etruscan Archaic Age (roughly corresponding to the Roman era known as the Monarchy, when kings ruled Rome). However, increasing evidence suggests that, despite their adoption of Greek-style heavy infantry, Etruscan armies lacked the tight organization and formidable power afforded by the phalanx. The reasons for this may have been political and social in nature. Most Greek hoplites (and Roman ones, too) were middle-class farmers who went to war to defend home and community.

The Etruscans failed to utilize the battlefield formations for which Greek armies were famous, including the phalanx (pictured).

They had a vested interest in doing so because they participated in government, even if only by taking part in debate in popular assemblies. In other words, a degree of democratization made Greek phalanxes what might today be called "bands of brothers," who stood by, and if necessary died for, one another when the going got tough.

In contrast, the tradition of aristocratic domination of the Etruscan armies, along with the cities and their governments, may well have made such comradeship and cohesion on the battlefield difficult and rare. Etruscan units may have assembled in phalanx fashion sometimes, when enough men with the proper armor could be found. But when facing a superior force, such units may have had a tendency to break down and disperse. Though scholars still debate it, this theory may explain why, when facing Roman armies in the centuries that followed, Etruscan ones almost always lost. As Barker and Rasmussen put it:

> The subsequent history of military conflict with Rome suggests that the Etruscans never adopted the Greek system in any thoroughgoing way,

whereas the Romans did, and Rome's large citizen army fighting in compact formation was inevitably superior.[20]

Etruscan Expansion

Still, in the Archaic Age, during most of which Rome was not yet a major player in Italian affairs, the Etruscans managed to make some headway into areas beyond Etruria. Sometime in the mid-500s B.C. colonizers from the Greek city of Phocaea founded a settlement on Corsica, the large island lying a few miles off the coast of Etruria. Believing that their local trade routes were threatened, two or more Etruscan cities made an alliance with the Carthaginians, who saw Corsica as part of their own trading sphere. In a large sea battle fought near the Corsican coast circa 535 B.C., the Etruscans and

Carthaginians won. In the aftermath the Phocaeans vacated Corsica and the Etruscans promptly built a settlement there.

About ten years later, Etruscan armies, perhaps from or led by Volterrae, moved northward across the Apennines into the region of modern Bologna. There they set up several small colonies. They also gained access to the Adriatic Sea at Spina and Adria, on the south and north sides of the Po River, respectively. This made trade with the peoples of the lands situated across the Adriatic (present-day Croatia) faster and easier.

At about the same time, Etruscan forces marched southward into the fertile region of Campania, bordering the Bay of Naples in southwestern Italy. There they took over some existing towns and established several new ones, the most important being Capua,

VICTORY AT SEA

In his *Histories*, the fifth-century B.C. Greek historian Herodotus gave this description of the sea battle fought circa 535 B.C. between the allied Etruscans and Carthaginians and the Greeks from Phocaea.

The Etruscans and Carthaginians agreed to attack them [the Phocaeans] with a fleet of sixty ships apiece. The Phocaeans manned their own vessels, also sixty in number, and sailed to meet them in the Sardinian Sea [i.e., the waters near Sardinia and Corsica]. . . . In the engagement that followed . . . forty of the [Phocaean] vessels were destroyed and the remaining twenty had their rams so badly bent as to render them unfit for service. The survivors returned to Alalia [their colony on Corsica], took aboard their women and children and such property as there was room for, and sailed from Corsica to Rhegium [in southern Italy]. The Carthaginians and Etruscans drew lots for the possession of the [Phocaean] prisoners from the ships that were sunk. . . . The Etruscans took them ashore and stoned them to death.

about twenty miles inland from the coast. This brought them into opposition with the Greeks at the coastal town of Cumae, then the major urban center in the area. A large battle took place near Cumae, though exactly how large is not known. It is also unclear exactly which Etruscan and Greek cities had troops involved. The outcome, however, is undisputed: The Etruscans lost and withdrew to their local strongholds. One of these seems to have been Pompeii on the slopes of Mount Vesuvius, then little more than a fishing village.

A few years later, perhaps about 506 B.C., an Etruscan army from Clusium, led by Arruns, son of Lars Porsenna, attacked the town of Aricia, north of Campania (and a few miles south of Rome). Remembering what had happened at Cumae, the Aricians appealed to the Cumaeans for help. Because Aricia was in Latium, a region dominated by Latin towns, a number of Latins joined forces with the Greeks to oppose Arruns. As Livy told it, at first the Etruscans broke the Latin lines. But then the Greeks "saved the day." They managed to outflank (move around and behind) the Etruscans, Livy said,

> then attacked them in the rear, with the result that the Etruscans were caught in a trap and cut to pieces almost in their moment of victory. Arruns was killed, and a handful of Etruscan soldiers, having nowhere nearer to go to, found their way to Rome, where they arrived unarmed and helpless and with no resource but to throw themselves on the Romans' mercy. They were kindly received and billeted [given places to sleep] in various houses.[21]

Rome Enters the Picture

The bloody episodes at Cumae and Aricia do more than show that the Etruscans encountered fierce resistance during their forays into southern Italy. These incidents also for the first time bring the young, up-and-coming city-state of Rome into the picture of Etruscan expansion beyond Etruria. Why did the Etruscans bypass, rather than attack and absorb, Rome on their way to Campania in the 520s B.C.? And why did the Romans, who were Latins, take in the Etruscan survivors of the battle at Aricia, where Etruscans opposed Latins?

Up until the last decades of the twentieth century, most scholars would have answered these questions by saying that at the time Rome was an Etruscan city. The prevailing theory was that sometime in the late Orientalizing Period or early Archaic Age the Etruscans conquered Rome. This seemed to explain the fact that the last few kings of Rome were of Etruscan birth, as well as the strong impact of Etruscan culture on Rome during this period. However, much doubt has been cast on this theory in recent years. In the era in question, Rome was a rapidly growing and cosmopolitan town that welcomed immigrants from numerous foreign cities. And many scholars now believe that the Etruscan kings of Rome were immigrants who rose to their positions through personal ability and initiative rather than by force of arms. According to noted scholar T.J. Cornell, compelling evidence

> suggests a process of emigration by small groups from individual Etruscan cities, who established themselves . . . as a significant element of the ruling class in settlements that already

BRAVE HORATIUS AT THE BRIDGE

According to Livy's history (in this excerpt from *Livy: The Early History of Rome*), as the army of Lars Porsenna approached Rome, it was delayed at the only bridge leading across the Tiber. A Roman patriot named Horatius, Livy said, held off the invaders single-handedly.

[As] the enemy forces came pouring down the hill . . . Horatius acted promptly. . . . Urging [his comrades] . . . to destroy the bridge by fire or steel or any means they could muster, he offered to hold up the Etruscan advance, so far as was possible, alone. Proudly he took his stand at the outer edge of the bridge. . . . He prepared himself for close combat, one man against an army. The advancing enemy paused in sheer astonishment at such reckless courage. . . . With defiance in his eyes Horatius confronted the [enemy], challenging one after the other to single combat and mocking them all. [Eventually, he jumped in the water and swam to safety.] It was a noble piece of work—legendary, maybe, but destined to be celebrated in story in the years to come.

In this illustration, Horatius repels invading Etruscans at Rome's Sublican bridge. The exploits of Horatius are likely greatly exaggerated.

existed as going concerns. In this way, they gained control of autonomous communities and pursued their own interests, rather than acting [under the direct orders] of a centralized Etruscan metropolis. That being the case, there was no need for . . . "the Etruscans" . . . to control Rome.[22]

This view of the situation in the Archaic Age would explain why Latin identity and culture remained predominant in Rome even under Etruscan kings. It would also explain why the Etruscans bypassed Rome on their way to Campania. Simply put, they viewed the regime there, with its Etruscan-

born rulers, as a friendly one and had no inclination to attack it. As for the refuge later given to the Etruscan stragglers from the battle against the Latins, strong mercantile and cultural ties had long existed between Rome and Etruria. And Livy mentions an "Etruscan quarter" in Rome (probably made up of Etruscan merchants and their families). It is not surprising, therefore, that at least some Romans were willing to aid the fugitives.

Regime Change in Rome

This is not to say that all Romans were ready and willing to be so generous to Etruscans at that moment. The fact is that the

Noted historian-artist Peter Connolly created this accurate reconstruction of Lars Porsenna and his troops preparing to attack Rome.

battle at Aricia occurred amid a momentous series of events in Roman history. About the year 509 B.C. (or perhaps slightly later), the regime of Rome's last Etruscan king, Tarquinius Superbus (or "Tarquin the Proud"), found itself in a major crisis. For several years, Tarquin's rule had become increasingly tyrannical. Among the abuses was his arrest of several wealthy Latin landowners on phony charges so that he could get their estates for himself.

Meanwhile, Tarquin's son, Sextus, got involved in various shady dealings that damaged and angered many leading citizens. Finally, Sextus raped Lucretia, wife of the noted aristocrat and patriot Lucius Tarquinius Collatinus. Collatinus, aided by another Roman notable, Lucius Junius Brutus, led a coup in which the Tarquins were locked out of the city. The leaders of the coup then abolished the kingship and established the Roman Republic, administered by men elected by the citizenry and advised by a group of senators.

However, the fledgling Republic now found *itself* in a serious crisis. The Etruscan city-states arrayed north of Rome had long been content to have a friendly, Etruscan-ruled Latin city on their southern flank. The ousting of the Tarquins suddenly changed the status quo. And the prospect of a strong, hostile Latin presence on Etruria's doorstep must have worried the leaders of the Etruscan states.

One of these leaders was Clusium's Lars Porsenna, who marched on Rome at the head of an army. He may have succeeded in occupying the city for a short time. (Recent excavations have revealed that several of Rome's important public buildings burned down about this time, which could be evidence of a violent takeover.) But it was not long before Porsenna was on his way back to Clusium. It is not known why or how he left Rome. But it is possible that, once he had taken the city, he decided to use it as a base from which to strike the Latin towns to the south. But then his son, Arruns, was disastrously defeated at Aricia, weakening Porsenna enough to force him to vacate Rome and retreat homeward.

Whatever the reasons for Porsenna's retreat, in a way it foreshadowed a more general Etruscan retreat and decline that would occur in the next two centuries. The city-states of Etruria had established numerous communities and trading posts beyond their traditional stomping grounds in Etruria. But they were not able to maintain these footholds for long. In addition to Romans and Greeks, other powerful Italian and non-Italian peoples were beginning to make bids for the same territories. And some had their eyes on Etruria itself.

ETRUSCAN CULTURE, ARTS, AND CRAFTS

Very few examples of Etruscan writing have survived. Yet ample evidence shows that a body of Etruscan literature, likely dominated by religious texts, did exist at one time. These writings and the highly distinct language used to create them were cultural aspects that set the Etruscans apart from their Greek and Latin neighbors. The fact that so little is known about the Etruscans' language and literature makes understanding their views of themselves and their world extremely difficult.

In a similar vein, relatively little is known about another important element of Etruscan culture—religion. Because they were constructed mainly of wood, Etruscan temples have long since disintegrated (in contrast to the survival of numerous more substantial stone Greek temples). And most of what little is known about Etruscan religious beliefs and practices comes from scattered remarks by later Greek and Roman writers. That so little is known about Etruscan religion is unfortunate because it appears that the Etruscans were an unusually pious people whose religious beliefs permeated all levels of their society.

Scholars are on somewhat firmer ground regarding the visual arts and practical crafts of the Etruscans. A number of well-preserved

examples of Etruscan pottery, painting, metalwork, and sculpture have survived, mostly in tombs. These reveal strong elements of Greek influence. This is not surprising, because so many other aspects of Etruscan culture—including gods, architecture, and language (thanks to the borrowing of the Greek alphabet)—were inspired by the Greeks. Yet the Etruscans were not mere copiers. All aspects of Etruscan culture involved a fusion of native and foreign elements, and scholars do their best to isolate and understand the native ones. Despite heavy Greek influences on Etruscan culture and arts, Ellen Macnamara points out,

> the differing personality and circumstances of the Etruscans . . . inevitably imposed a quite individual treatment of these art forms. Although they may follow Greek styles . . . the Etruscans used them for their own requirements and within a regional interpretation, often that of a single city-state.[23]

Moreover, many surviving Etruscan arts and crafts contain tantalizing hints of a decidedly non-Greek view of how art should relate to and reflect the world, society, and everyday life. "The Greeks sought to express the sublime and the eternal through harmony and idealization, especially of the human body," Macnamara writes. Thus, classical Greek statues often show figures having ideal, perfect physical form, works meant to convey general ideas of what is good and beautiful in all times and places. In contrast, Macnamara continues,

> The Etruscans seemed disinterested in generalization and in abstract ideas and so used the Greek forms to convey their own inclinations toward the particular

and the personal, often emphasizing the temporary [aspects of life] and [in] expressive detail. It is for this [uniquely Etruscan] reinterpretation and self-expression that we must chiefly look in studying Etruscan art and [culture].[24]

A Different Tongue

It is fitting to begin the search for the more distinctly native elements of the Etruscans' culture by examining what is known about their language and writing. After all, the Etr-

The Etruscans had no large religious temples before the influx of Greek influences into Etruria. Pictured is a replica of an Etruscan temple.

ORIGINS OF THE
ETRUSCAN LANGUAGE

Most of the languages of Europe belong to a large family of languages that experts call Indo-European. However, Etruscan, along with Finnish, Hungarian, and Basque, does not belong to this family. Besides Etruria, the only other ancient place where scholars have found evidence for the Etruscan tongue (actually what seems to be a dialect of it) is on the island of Lemnos, in the northern Aegean Sea. This discovery was one of the reasons that most scholars long suspected that the Etruscans migrated to Italy from the eastern Mediterranean, a notion that is now rejected. (Indeed, such evidence could just as well support the idea that a group of Etruscans migrated from Italy to Lemnos in the dim past.)

Although the origins of Etruscan remain unclear, it is plausible that its roots are very ancient and that it is native to Italy and/or nearby regions. An early version of it may have been spoken there and elsewhere in the Mediterranean basin before the arrival of Indo-European speakers in the area in the third and second millennia B.C.

uscan language was decidedly different from the tongues of all the peoples the Etruscans dealt with. In fact, scholars are reasonably sure that Etruscan was not in the great Indo-European family of related languages, as were Greek, Celtic (northern European), Latin, and Umbrian (central Italian). The origins of Etruscan are unknown. But the current scholarly consensus is that it was one of a group of non-Indo-European languages spoken in the Mediterranean basin in prehistoric times. According to this view, Etruscan was the only tongue in this group that survived into the first millennium B.C.

Borrowing from Other Cultures

There is no doubt that Etruscan continued to change in that era, as it borrowed words and phrases from Latin, Greek, and perhaps other languages. Yet it remained largely alien to these tongues. This explains why, after adopting the Greek alphabet, the Etruscans immediately dropped the signs for d, b, g, and o. Apparently they were unnecessary to expressing Etruscan words. Another alien aspect of Etruscan was that it was written from right to left, instead of left to right, as are Greek and Latin, and of course English. (This quirk spilled over into the visual arts, in which the narrative flow of paintings on walls and pottery vessels ran in the opposite direction to that of Greek paintings).

In the seventh century B.C., when they were just breaking in their newly borrowed alphabet, few Etruscans could read and write. Inscriptions of this period appear almost exclusively in upper-class tombs, and it seems as though reading skills were at first a form of class distinction. The evidence suggests "a symbolic, perhaps even magical, importance," Barker and Rasmussen write, "by which those who had access to this new power were separated out from those who did not."[25] In the two following centuries, however, the number of inscriptions increased dramatically and were not restricted to the wealthiest tombs. This suggests that writing skills had spread to the members of the middle class that grew as a result of Etruscan expansion and prosperity in the Archaic Age.

Today, scholars struggle to understand the words and phrases these long lost people took for granted. So far, the names of people, gods, several mythological heroes, and some months of the year have been translated. The terms for "father" and "daughter" are known, as are the names of some kinds of common vases and other containers. (A cup with two vertical handles was called a *χavena*, for example.) And some Etruscan numbers are readable. But much needs to be done before the Etruscan language is truly readable and gives up the many secrets it holds about its original speakers.

Gods and Religious Beliefs

Like the Etruscan language, the religion of the people of Etruria was affected by contact with the Greeks yet retained certain distinctive native qualities. Before the infusion of Greek influence, it appears that the Etruscans practiced a form of animism. Generally speaking, this is a belief system in which divine forces are spirits that possess vague, nonhuman form and inhabit most

parts of nature, including trees, rocks, and water. The early Romans also practiced animism, and it is possible that they learned it from the Etruscans.

By contrast, the Greeks worshipped anthropomorphized gods, that is, deities viewed as having human form, emotions, and agendas. The Etruscans were so taken with Greek culture that they swiftly applied this idea to many of their traditional divinities. For instance, the formless Etruscan sky god Tinia came to be seen in human form as the equivalent of Zeus (the Roman Jupiter), leader of the Greek gods. The Etruscan spirit Uni became associated with Zeus's wife, Hera; the

This carved head is an Etruscan representation of the Greek god Zeus, whom the Etruscans called Tinia.

Etruscan Fufluns with the fertility god Dionysus; the Etruscan Sethlans with Hephaestos, god of the forge; the Etruscan Menerva with Athena, goddess of wisdom and war; and so forth. (The Roman goddess Minerva, also equivalent to Athena, was likely a borrowing of the Etruscan Menerva.)

Despite this "humanization" of many (though certainly not all) Etruscan divinities, certain aspects of Etruscan religion did not conform to Greek ideas of the divine. For one thing, as Michael Grant points out, the Etruscans had "a far stronger sense of their subordination to the will of the heavenly powers." To an Etruscan, the gods were not only omnipotent but also in complete control of human destiny. In addition, Grant says, the Etruscans

> retained a sort of magical, mystical, illogical interpretation of phenomena which the Greeks had early begun to discard in favor of a gradually strengthening rationalism [and modern-style scientific outlook] that remained meaningless to the Etruscans.[26]

Because the Etruscans perceived a divine hand and meaning in practically everything that happened, they worried even more than the Greeks did about divine wrath. Indeed, there was a major emphasis in Etruscan culture not only on appeasing the gods but also on interpreting the divine will and predicting future events preordained by the gods. For this reason, the Etruscans became famous for their ability to interpret omens and other divine signs. The importance the Romans placed on such divine interpretation (called divination) apparently came from their cultural contacts with the Etruscans. And Roman leaders continued to

respect and rely on Etruscan diviners long after Rome had conquered and absorbed the Etruscan states.

There were several different types of Etruscan diviners. Some specialized in reading the supposed meanings inherent in flashes of lightning, cloud formations, bird flight patterns, and other natural displays. The Roman/Latin word for such an expert was *auger*. Another kind of diviner inspected the livers of animals that were slaughtered during the ritual of sacrifice. The Romans called such a person a *haruspex*. (The equivalent Etruscan word seems to have been *netsvis*.) Barker and Rasmussen provide this excellent summary of how a *haruspex* worked:

> The surface of the liver was viewed as if it were the sky above in microcosm [miniature], so that it became in effect another means of consulting the sky gods. This required [a good deal of] precision and it mattered greatly how the organ was held in relation to the sky and where on its surface any irregularities were located. On the famous bronze model of a sheep's liver [found at] Piacenza [on the Po River, north of Etruria], the surface is divided into numerous compartments, each, like the sky itself, "inhabited" by a god whose name is incised. . . . The whole system was so complex that even a trained *haruspex* might have needed a crib [cheat sheet] of this sort by him fairly constantly.[27]

Conceptions of the afterlife was another religious area in which native Etruscan and Greek ideas merged. Before Greek contact, the Etruscans seem to have believed in some sort of afterlife, but the nature of this belief

A wall painting from the Tomb of the Augurs. The Etruscans were famous for their augurs, who supposedly could interpret divine signs.

and their visions of what lay beyond death are uncertain. Some evidence suggests that they thought the gods judged humans to be either worthy or unworthy of enjoying the afterlife and that performing certain rituals on a regular basis would ensure salvation. Later, especially from the fourth century B.C. on, Greek conceptions of the afterlife and Underworld became predominant in the art in Etruscan tombs. In this view, the souls of the dead made their way to the Underworld, presided over by the god Aita (the Etruscan version of the Greek Hades). There, some led happy lives in pleasant surroundings, while others wandered aimlessly across a featureless, dismal plain.

At the same time, Etruscan demons became prominent in tomb art. The most important of these frightful creatures was Charun, who wielded a huge hammer with which he bludgeoned the souls of the unworthy. (The Romans borrowed this character. Armed men costumed to represent Charun closely checked fallen gladiators in the arena and brutally killed any who were pretending to be dead.)

Temples and Other Large-Scale Architecture

Besides various forms of divination, the other religious rituals the Etruscans performed are not fully understood. But overall

SOME IMPORTANT ETRUSCAN GODS

This chart shows the Etruscan equivalents, where applicable, of some important Greek and Roman deities.

Etruscan Name	Function	Greek Equivalent	Roman Equivalent
Aita	lord of the Underworld	Hades	Pluto or Dis
Ani	beginnings	none	Janus
Aplu	thunder and lightning	Apollo	Apollo
Artumes	night, death, fertility	Artemis	Diana
Charun	demon who torments souls	none	none
Fufluns	vegetation, mirth, fertility	Dionysus	Bacchus
Lasa	goddesses who guard graves of believers	none	none
Menerva	knowledge, war, justice	Athena	Minerva
Nethuns	wells, the seas	Poseidon	Neptune
Sethlans	fire, forges	Hephaestos	Vulcan
Tinia	sky, supreme god	Zeus	Jupiter
Turan	love, health	Aphrodite	Venus
Turms	messenger god, protector of trades	Hermes	Mercury
Uni	Tinia's wife, supreme goddess	Hera	Juno
Voltumna	change, seasons	none	none

they were probably not much different than those of the Greeks and Romans. The main Greco-Roman ritual was sacrifice, usually of animals but also of vegetation and liquids (called libations). These offerings were intended to nourish and thereby appease the gods. Evidence shows that the Etruscans, too, performed regular sacrifices.

The subject of rituals naturally brings religious temples, and of necessity large-scale architecture, into the discussion. Before contact with the Greeks, the Etruscans had no temples. Their rituals were performed in open-air sanctuaries (sacred grounds), each of which had one or more altars for sacrifice. Beginning about 600 B.C. or so, however,

under the influence of the Greeks, the Etruscan city-states started erecting large temples. As was true in Greek cities, these structures served two main purposes—to house a larger-than-life-sized statue (the "cult image") of a god and to enhance the civic pride and overall prestige of the city that built such an expensive and impressive building. (To respect the god's privacy, since it was thought that he or she actually dwelled in the temple from time to time, no worship took place inside these structures.)

Although the architecture of Etruscan temples was strongly influenced by Greek models, there were several important differences. First, the vast majority, if not all, of

This model of an Etruscan temple shows the low-sloping roof and other design features that differed from those of Greek temples.

the Etruscan versions were made of wood instead of stone, making them impermanent. This choice of material may have been dictated by the lack of good building stone in Etruria (and conversely, the ready supply of excellent timber). Second, only a few Etruscan temples copied the Greek style of surrounding the inner sanctum with colonnades (rows of columns). Most Etruscan versions had far fewer columns and only in the front; the sides and back of such a structure consisted of plain walls. Also, the roof of an Etruscan temple was lower and had less pitch than its Greek counterpart. And whereas a typical Greek temple had one or two interior main rooms, *cellas*, most Etruscan temples had three smaller interior *cellae*, plus wings (*alae*) on the sides. The first-century B.C. Roman architect Vitruvius saw many Etruscan temples firsthand and, fortunately for later generations, gave a detailed description of their proper layout. It reads in part:

> The place where the temple is to be built having been divided on its length into six parts, deduct one and let the rest be given to its width. Then let the length be divided into two equal parts, of which let the inner be reserved as space for the *cellae*, and the part next to the front left for the arrangement of the columns. Next let the width be divided into ten parts. Of these, let three on the right and three on the left be given to the smaller *cellae*, or to the *alae* if there are to be *alae*, and the other four devoted to the middle of the temple. Let the space in front of the *cellae*, in the pronaos [front area or porch], be marked out for columns.[28]

Of other examples of Etruscan monumental architecture, the larger tombs are the most impressive that survive. Very few buildings from the Etruscan cities have been excavated to date, so it is possible that they featured other large-scale public structures besides temples and tombs. The Etruscans certainly built roads and bridges that were impressive for their time. During the seventh and sixth centuries B.C., a considerable network of roads connected the major Etruscan cities, ports, and cemeteries. Some of these roads were made of dirt or dirt covered by gravel, but other sections were cut directly out of the volcanic *tufo* that covers much of Etruria. One surviving cutting still bears the name of its engineer—Larth Vel Arnies—carved in the *tufo*.

Most of the bridges that carried these roads over streams were made of wood and have long since vanished. However, the remains of a bridge at San Giovanale, near Tarquinii, show what some of the better Etruscan bridges were like. Two huge bridge supports made of *tufo*, one on each side of a stream and nearly seventy feet apart, are still extant. And remnants of stone pillars in the stream indicate that a series of stone supports held up the middle sections of a massive timber roadway that forded the stream.

Pottery and Painting

Remains of smaller-scale but no less impressive examples of Etruscan culture also survive. Among these artifacts are numerous pottery vessels. The prevailing style of Etruscan pottery in the Villanovan period was a coarse type that modern scholars call impasto. For a long time it was fashioned by hand without a potter's wheel and heated in an open fire. To give the pots extra strength,

BLACK-FIGURE POTTERY

Much of the pottery used in Etruria in ancient times was imported from Greece. This included a great deal of ceramic ware from Athens, particularly in the black-figure style. In this tract from her book *The Etruscans*, scholar Ellen Macnamara describes the black-figure technique.

Clay with a quantity of iron oxide in its composition may be fired black or red, according to the temperature and amount of oxygen allowed into the kiln on firing. The "paint" used by the Greeks to decorate their black-figured vases was in fact a purified and liquid form of the same clay used to create the vessel and, by a complicated sequence of temperature changes, together with the varying amount of oxygen allowed into the kiln during a single firing, Greek potters ensured that the body of the vessel was fired red, while the painted figures and other decorations were fired black. In black-figure technique, the figures are painted in silhouette with inner details incised [scraped with a pointed tool] or added in color.

the artisans mixed the clay with tiny chips of rock or ground-up pottery shards. Decoration was usually minimal.

Impasto ware, which increased in quality over time, continued to be produced in the Orientalizing Period and Archaic Age. However, it was largely overshadowed by two new general types, one native and one foreign. The foreign type, of course, was Greek. At first, Corinthian pottery was the most popular import, but by the middle of the sixth century B.C. the work of Athenian artists predominated. The new native Etruscan type is today termed *bucchero*. It was made using a potter's wheel (adopted from the Greeks) and baked in a kiln (which produces higher temperatures than an open fire). The baking process purposely restricted the inflow of oxygen, which gave the pots a black color. This technique may have been partly designed to produce a metallic look, since metal containers were more expensive and more coveted. "*Bucchero* is pottery pretending to be metalware," says Nigel Spivey.

From the earliest example, it looks as though the initial intention was to glaze and fire *bucchero* to a fine metallic sheen. If modes of decoration more commonly found in metalwork . . . are added . . . the result can be almost convincing.[29]

Many Etruscan and Greek pottery containers were painted with designs, scenes of everyday life, or both. Etruscan artists also painted the inside walls of many of their tombs beginning in the early seventh century

B.C. Veii and Caere appear to have led the way, and neighboring cities quickly followed suit. (In subsequent centuries the artists of Tarquinii became the acknowledged masters of the art.) The most common variety was the fresco, a painting done on wet plaster. As Macnamara explains:

> The walls of tombs hewn from the rock were smoothed and covered with plaster. . . . The scene was quickly sketched in . . . painted outlines, and then while the plaster was still wet, the paint was filled in. In this technique, the paint sinks into the plaster, and as long as the plaster survives, so does the painting.[30]

Sculpture and Metalwork

Etruscan painting was often complemented by sculptures. Unlike the Greeks, the Etruscans produced very little stone sculpture, concentrating instead on bronze and terra-cotta (baked clay). Etruscan artists were renowned throughout the Mediterranean world for their fine metalware. They produced many exquisite items of bronze, including mirrors, vases, pitchers, plates, and so forth. They were also known for their gold items, including all manner of jewelry. In addition, Etruscan artisans evidently made large bronze statues, but the vast majority of these were later melted down by the Romans and others to salvage the metal. A number of beautiful small bronze figurines have survived, however, and

give some idea of how magnificent the larger versions must have been.

Etruscan terra-cotta sculptures display an equally high degree of expertise. One of the two main modes of terra-cotta work was the creation of decorations for the roofs of

Pictured are Etruscan valuables, including a gold statuette, a necklace with a pendant attached, a ring, and a brooch.

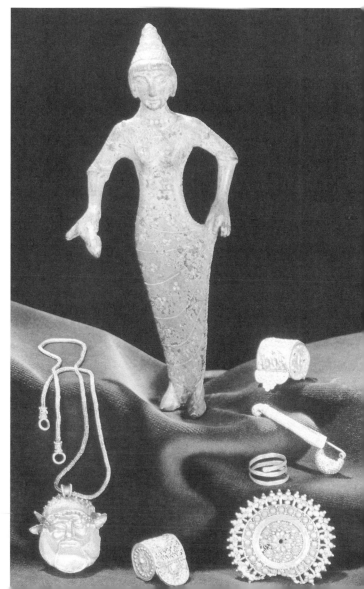

temples and houses. Stylistically speaking, these works were strongly influenced by the work of Greek sculptors, especially Athenian ones. The only native Etruscan artist whose name has survived—Vulca of Veii— was a master of terra-cotta sculpture and was reported to have created a splendid statue of Jupiter for the Romans in the sixth century B.C. The other main mode of Etruscan terra-cotta sculpture was the production of figures of deceased persons (in some cases life-sized) atop their terra-cotta or stone coffins. Sometimes a single person was depicted, but often

couples, usually husband and wife, were shown reclining together in a leisurely pose.

Overall, as time went on, native Etruscan styles of architecture, pottery, painting, metalware, and sculpture increasingly lost their distinctive character. At first, they merged with Greek styles. And eventually they adopted Roman ones (which had themselves been transformed by Greek models). By the first century A.D., Etruscan arts, crafts, and culture, along with the Etruscan language, had largely disappeared into the Greco-Roman cultural melting pot.

CHAPTER FIVE

ETRUSCAN HOMES, SOCIETY, AND LEISURE ACTIVITIES

Because most Etruscan literature has vanished and so few Etruscan cities and houses have been excavated to date, scholars are hard-pressed to reconstruct Etruscan society. Some information about family life, social customs, clothing styles, and leisure activities has come from studies of paintings and other artifacts found in Etruscan tombs; and Greek and Roman writers mentioned a few customs the Etruscans supposedly passed on to the Romans. But for the most part, Etruscan home life, social classes and customs, political offices and institutions, and other aspects of everyday life must be pieced together using scattered clues and educated guesswork.

Etruscan Houses

Various clues from the excavated tombs, for example, give some indication of what Etruscan houses were like. In some cases, it appears that the inner chambers of tombs were purposely laid out to reflect the layout of local houses. (And this same pattern is repeated in the ground plans of the Etruscan temples described by Vitruvius.) The most common layout is rectangular and has a front hall, or foyer, which leads to a cluster of three rooms in the back. Walls were made of stone or timber or both, and roofs were composed of timber beams covered by terracotta tiles. Such houses are known from some excavated Roman towns, including Pompeii (which had been an Etruscan town for a while in its early years). In fact, some scholars think that the Romans borrowed this basic house plan from the Etruscans. The Romans called the front hall, used by the master of the house to greet his guests, the atrium.

Evidence suggests that as time went on the Etruscans increasingly adopted Greek concepts of city planning and house plans. This can be seen in the remains of the town of Marzabotto, established north of Etruria during a phase of Etruscan expansion in the late sixth century B.C. (toward the end of the Archaic Age). Following Greek models, the streets were laid out in a rectangular grid forming city blocks a little more than five hundred feet long. Each block had seven or eight houses. The layouts varied, but most had a central, unroofed courtyard with a series of rooms (sometimes on two stories) organized around it.

It is likely, though by no means certain, that these types of houses were those of Etruscans of average means. Poorer, less substantial huts similar to those of the Villanovan period still existed in the Archaic Age and

Etruscan homes featured chests as storage space. This chest is fashioned in the shape of a typical house.

beyond, especially in the countryside. At the same time, aristocratic Etruscans could afford much larger and more elaborate homes. A very spacious and luxurious home has been excavated at Murlo, a few miles southeast of Volterrae. Following clues found in the ruins, archaeologists believe it was first built in around 650 B.C., eventually suffered destruction by fire, and was rebuilt about 575 B.C. on an even more splendid scale. The house, which may have been the minor palace of a local leader, has four large wings clustered around a central courtyard that measures some 180 feet across. The courtyard originally featured an impressive colonnade on its perimeter, and the house was filled with high-quality wall frescoes and terra-cotta statues.

Authority Figures and Their Symbols

Clearly, as was true among the Greeks, Romans, and other ancient peoples, most Etruscans were not fortunate enough to live like the master of the Murlo mansion. Few Etruscan country houses have been excavated so far. But it is likely that most were humble, simple abodes and that a majority of Etruscans dwelled in such homes in rural villages and farms. Unfortunately, the majority of these small houses were made of perishable materials that have left little or no trace.

Though disappointed, archaeologists and historians are not surprised. They have repeatedly found that the vast bulk of the surviving evidence, both physical and literary, for ancient cultures is for wealthy, powerful people who lived in well-built structures and monopolized the attention of ancient writers.

The palacelike house at Murlo not only underscores the vast gulf between rich and poor in ancient Etruria but also raises the question of who ruled the Etruscan city-states and what the governments of these states were like. There was no single king or other leader who ruled over all the Etruscan states. It has already been established that the meetings of representatives of these states, held perhaps annually at Voltumna, were religious in nature. It is likely that athletic games and market-fairs were part of the festivities at such gatherings. Also, the leaders from the various city-states probably socialized and exchanged opinions about the issues of the day.

But these leaders, like the city-states themselves, consistently remained autonomous. At first they were kings, the Etruscan word for which seems to have been *lauchum* (*lucumo* in Latin). The king probably directly controlled the military, local justice, and the state religion. An idea of the symbols of an Etruscan king's powers can be seen indirectly in certain later Roman customs. According to Livy and other Roman historians, the Romans borrowed a number of such symbols from the Etruscans. One was the use of lictors, attendants who accompanied the Etruscan kings (and some powerful Roman magistrates). Etruscan and Roman lictors carried the fasces (from which the modern

ARCHAEOLOGICAL REMAINS OF ETRUSCAN FARMS

As was the case in other ancient Mediterranean lands, most of the inhabitants of Etruria were farmers who lived in modest huts or small houses. Archaeologists have found the remains of a number of bronze, iron, and terra-cotta farm implements and artifacts that give some idea of Etruscan agricultural methods. A farmer tilled the soil using a plow constructed of a wooden frame tipped with an iron point, or he used an iron pick very similar to the kind still used by Italian peasant farmers. The ancient farmers harvested their grain with sharpened bronze sickles and loaded it into wooden wagons pulled by oxen. Most farms probably had small barns for storing foodstuffs (in large pottery containers that the Greeks called amphorae) and tools. Some farms had large sunken storage jars for storing fermenting wine. And remnants of what seem to have been presses for crushing grapes or olives have been found. Another excavation has revealed the remains of a workroom where cheese was produced from sheep's milk.

These detailed carvings of lictors are only four inches high. The Romans borrowed the concept of lictors from the Etruscans.

word *fascism* derives). Consisting of a bundle of branches and rods with a double-headed ax at the center, the fasces signified the kingly authority to execute any and all transgressors. Other regal symbols the Romans took from the Etruscans included the toga with the purple border (purple being the traditional color of royalty in ancient times); the custom of giving a victorious military leader a triumph (victory parade); and perhaps even the eagle, a major symbol of both the Roman Republic and Empire.

The Etruscan kings occupied the highest place in the aristocracies of their respective cities. And it is possible that a few very wealthy families monopolized power in each city for generations. Yet some evidence suggests that by the end of the Archaic Age power in at least some of these cities had passed to oligarchies (from Greek words meaning "rule of the few"). There is no evidence to suggest that they were democratic-style councils, like the ones that developed in many Greek cities and in Rome. Indeed, the Etruscan versions were likely still dominated by aristocrats. But these councils of magistrates either replaced or shared authority with the kings. The names of the offices of some of the magistrates—*zilath*, *purth*, and *maru*—have been found in inscriptions in tombs. However, exactly what the *zilath* and other officials did and the extent of their powers remain unknown.

Social Classes: Women

The breakdown of social classes among the people ruled by the kings, *zilath*, and other authority figures is also sketchy. One certain fact is that family units, both the immediate family and the larger clan, were central to Etruscan society. Evidence from the tombs shows that family ties, even with long-dead relatives, were highly revered and a source of great pride. The names of relatives, both living and deceased, were carefully listed in a person's grave. Typical is the tomb of Lars Pulenas at Tarquinii, in which a terra-cotta

statue of him holds a scroll (also of terra-cotta) bearing the names of his father, uncle, grandfather, and great-grandfather.

It was also a common Etruscan custom to list the name of a deceased person's mother in a tomb. This leads into the fascinating subject of Etruscan women and the unusually high degree of social status and freedom they apparently enjoyed (as compared with most Greek and Roman women). Besides the listing of women's names in tombs, other archaeological evidence indicates that Etruscan women (at least those in the upper classes, since most of the evidence is about them) enjoyed a degree of social freedom unheard-of in most neighboring lands. Tomb sculptures and paintings show women

This wall painting shows a procession of women at an Etruscan funeral. Etruscan women enjoyed more personal freedom than Greek women.

This sculpted head of an Etruscan woman dates from the fourth century B.C.

Greek woman spent most of her time at home, was not allowed to attend dinner parties given by her husband, and had to retire to the "women's quarters" in the back of the house when men from outside the family were visiting.

In comparison, Roman women were not quite as subservient and marginalized as Greek women were. Still, both Greek and Roman writers, almost all of them men, were harshly critical of Etruscan women, whose lives they saw as much too free and permissive. Typical was the following passage by the fourth-century B.C. Greek historian Theopompus:

> It is normal for the Etruscans to share their women in common. These women take great care of their bodies and exercise bare, exposing their bodies even before men and among themselves, for it is not shameful for them to appear almost naked. . . . The Etruscans raise all the children that are born, not knowing who the father is of each one. The children eventually live like those who brought them up, and have many drinking parties, and they too make love with all the women. It is no shame for Etruscans to be seen [in public] having sexual experiences. . . . They make love sometimes within sight of each other.[31]

dining, attending sporting contests, and sharing in other activities equally with men.

That does not mean that Etruscan women had the same political rights as men. As in the vast majority of ancient societies, women in Etruria could not hold public office or any positions of real power. Yet there is no doubt that socially speaking they were considerably more liberated than the women of the Greek cities of southern Italy in Archaic times and the age that followed. While the treatment of women varied somewhat from one Greek area to another, in general Greek women were socially subservient to men and lived narrow and strictly controlled lives. The average

No direct evidence supporting such biased and distorted views of supposed Etruscan promiscuity and immorality has been found. In fact, the archaeological record seems actually to contradict such negative and titillating allegations. "The evidence of the monuments," Ellen Macnamara writes,

> amply demonstrates . . . that Theopompus's charges are no more than salacious gossip. Not only do the funerary inscriptions show a very strong pride in the family, but a clear idea of married love is expressed in effigies [carved images] of affectionate married couples, which we see on some of the sarcophagi [stone coffins].[32]

There is an interesting footnote connected to female Etruscan liberation. Namely, adverse Greco-Roman reactions to Etruscan liberality, and Roman dislike of the Etruscans in general, may partly explain why the Romans imposed limits on their own women over the course of time. A number of scholars suggest that very early in Rome's history women had inheritance rights similar to men's, but by the advent of the Republic (in the late Etruscan Archaic Age) women had lost most of these rights. If this did indeed happen, it may support the following scenario. At first, Roman women gained a number of social rights through the enlightened influence of the Etruscans. Then, in establishing the Republic, the Romans threw out their Etruscan-born king and his courtiers, an act likely accompanied by a general negative reaction to overt Etruscan ideas and customs. Anxious to demonstrate to the world that Rome was not and never had been an Etruscan city, male Roman leaders tightened their control over Roman women.

Social Classes: Clients, Freedmen, and Slaves

Although the preceding scenario remains unproven, there is little doubt that certain other

Roman social customs were adopted from or strongly influenced by those of Etruria. Evidence suggests, for instance, that Etruscan society had a deep-rooted patronage system like that of Rome. In Rome, patronage was a society-wide institution in which upper-class or well-off patrons enjoyed the support of lower-class and less-well-off clients. Clients did errands and favors for their patrons and supported them in both public events and private business dealings; in exchange, the patrons gave legal, financial, or other kinds of protection to the clients.

The existence of this system, which benefited poorer folk to some degree, may well explain why the Etruscan lower classes tolerated the dominance of the aristocracy and a few privileged families for as long as they did. They did not tolerate it forever, however. Eventually, class warfare like the kind that had occurred in Rome and many Greek cities centuries before rocked some of the Etruscan city-states. According to Livy, in 302 B.C. such disturbances took place at Arretium, where "a movement had begun to force out the all-powerful family of the Cilnii, because of the envy aroused by their wealth."[33] A generation later, at Volsinii, a group of former slaves, who had long worked as assistants and overseers for the local elite, pushed that elite out and took over the government.

The "former slaves" at Volsinii belonged to a social class beneath that of the aristocrats and middle class, namely the freedmen. In the ancient world, a freedman was a male or female slave who had managed to gain his or her freedom in some manner. (Sometimes a master freed a slave as a reward for years of loyal service; also, many slaves received regular allowances, and some saved up the

The bound, naked man in this Etruscan wall painting seems to be a war prisoner. Such people usually became slaves.

money and bought their freedom.) In Greece, Rome, and Etruria as well, freedmen were often artisans, shopkeepers, farm overseers, secretaries, and other responsible workers who did jobs that the elite felt were beneath their dignity. The name given to freedmen in Etruscan inscriptions was *lautni* (as compared to the Latin *libertus*). Once freed, an Etruscan freedman customarily took one of his or her former master's names and became a loyal client.

Below the freedmen, of course, were the slaves. Almost nothing is known about Etruscan slaves, except that there were rela-

tively large numbers of them and that they did all of society's menial and unpleasant jobs. These included mining, quarrying, street cleaning, agricultural labor, household cleaning and maintenance, and so forth. Evidence from tombs shows that the slaves were addressed only by their first names and were not allowed to use the family name, as freedmen were.

Clothing and Hairstyles

Though the evidence for Etruscan politics and social classes remains sketchy, that for clothes and hairstyles is fairly extensive.

This is because many surviving vase and wall paintings show what Etruscan men and women looked like. Like other peoples in the ancient Mediterranean world, the inhabitants of Etruria generally wore loosely draped garments. As a rule, these consisted of an inner layer—the simple tunic (sometimes worn by itself)—and an outer cloak or wrap. The Etruscan word for the outer garment was *tebenna*. Both the tunic and outer wrap were usually made of either linen or wool, perhaps depending on the season (wool being warmer in cooler weather).

The style of these clothes changed over time, as happens in all cultures. In the seventh century B.C., Etruscan women wore ankle-length tunics, usually with belts at the waist, and a rectangular *tebenna* held in place at the shoulder by a decorative brooch. Their hair was long and braided. The men also wore a long tunic and were clean shaven, with their hair reaching to their shoulders.

Not surprisingly, in the sixth century B.C. Greek-style fashions were the rage in the Etruscan lands. Some men continued to wear long tunics, but many adopted the Greek custom of donning only a loincloth and going bare-chested. Also common was a short cloak that a man threw over his left shoulder but wound under his right one, leaving the right arm free. Men's hair was now longer and most men sported beards,

The woman depicted in this Etruscan tomb sculpture clearly shows her tebenna, *or cloak.*

EVIDENCE FOR ETRUSCAN SYMPOSIA

In ancient Greece, an after-dinner drinking party was called a symposium. (Two writers, Plato and Xenophon, wrote treatises with this title in which the guests at such a party engage in conversations, and numerous vase paintings show scenes from symposia.) The main evidence for Etruscan versions of symposia takes the form of paintings found in tombs, especially those near Tarquinii (including the so-called tombs of the Black Sow, Jugglers, Leopards, Ship, Lionesses, and Cockerel). These paintings show party guests reclining on comfortable wooden couches, usually resting on their left arms (indicating that most were right-handed). Often prominent is a large bowl (*krater*) for mixing wine with water, a custom practiced by the Greeks, Romans, and Etruscans alike. Some paintings show a sort of liquor cabinet equipped with cups, ladles, strainers, and other drinking accessories. Still other scenes depict party guests playing games such as *cottabos* and enjoying music, dancing, and other entertainment.

like those of the Greeks in this period. Etruscan women, meanwhile, still wore long tunics. But they now wore their hair in long, carefully wound ringlets, some of which fell forward over their shoulders. They also often wore headbands and a tall domed hat called a *tutulus*. Both men and women wore pointed shoes (made of black or colored leather) and finely made sandals (some with bronze soles).

In the centuries that followed (encompassing the Classical and Hellenistic eras), men cut their hair shorter and got rid of their beards. Women also wore their hair shorter (often above the ears), and some bleached it blond. Long tunics remained fashionable for both sexes, but these garments were now often sleeveless, belted above the waist, and brightly colored. The Roman-style toga also became common for formal

wear among Etruscan aristocrats in these centuries.

Banquets and Dancing

In the surviving paintings, the Etruscans wearing these handsome outfits are often depicted enjoying various leisure activities. One of the most popular of all was the banquet, or dinner party, which was equally popular in Roman and Greek cities. For an upper-class Etruscan, giving such parties was a way to display one's high status, as well as to reward and maintain the loyalty of one's dependent clients. The paintings frequently show the diners reclining on couches.

In general, Etruscan dinner parties featured lots of drinking, carousing, and entertainment (musicians, dancers, jugglers, and perhaps acrobats). One major difference was that Etruscan women were allowed to attend such gatherings, whereas most women were banned from the Greek versions. (An exception was prostitutes, whom Greek custom allowed men to invite.) Paintings are not the only artistic venue that show Etruscan couples partying. It became a common Etruscan burial custom to adorn a coffin with a terracotta sculpture of the deceased husband and wife reclining together, a moment of happiness frozen forever in time.

At dinner parties and in other situations, dancers were very popular entertainers in Etruria. Many kinds of Etruscan dances are depicted in paintings and sculptures, the earliest being military in nature. These military dances appear to have been similar to the Greek Pyrrhic dance, in which several young men, either nude or lightly clad, went through a series of precise moves in unison while wielding weapons and shields. Dancing, perhaps including impersonations of mythological characters, also took place during religious ceremonies. The Etruscans became famous for their dance acts, which other peoples, among them the Romans, sometimes imported for their own ceremonies. "Players were brought [into Rome] from Etruria," Livy wrote,

> to dance to the strains of the pipe without any singing or miming of song, and made quite graceful movements

A painted scene from the Tomb of the Augurs shows wrestlers grappling. Wrestling was one of many sporting events the Etruscans enjoyed.

in the Etruscan style. Then the young Romans began to copy them, exchanging jokes at the same time in crude improvised verse, with gestures to fit the words. Thus, the [Etruscan] entertainment was adopted and became established by frequent repetition. The native actors were called *histriones*, because the Etruscan word for an actor-dancer is *ister*.[34]

Leisure Activities

Other popular forms of entertainment among the Etruscans included party and parlor games, athletics, and leisure sports. One popular party game that caught on in Etruria's Hellenistic Age (beginning about 300 B.C.) was the Greek game called *cottabos*. There were several versions, but in the most common one the partiers took turns tossing the wine dregs at the bottoms of their cups at some sort of target. The person who managed to hit the target first was the winner. The Etruscans also played board games that may have been similar to modern checkers and chess; evidence for lined boards and carved wooden playing pieces have been found. In addition, they enjoyed gambling-style games, including throwing dice (which they also used in fortune-telling) and knucklebones

A BRUTAL SPORT

No actual accounts of Etruscan boxing matches have survived. But evidence suggests that the hand gear, moves, and outcomes were very similar to those of Greek matches. The following Greek account from the third century B.C. (quoted in Waldo E. Sweet's *Sport and Recreation in Ancient Greece*) underscores the brutality involved in a sport in which serious injuries were common and some men were literally beaten to death.

All the [spectators] shouted in unison, when they saw the damage Amykos had suffered around his mouth and jaw. As his face swelled, his eyes started to close. Then Polydeuces . . . confused his opponent by feinting [pretending to move] from all directions. And when he saw that Amykos was confused, he smashed his fist into his opponent's brow, right over the nose, and opened up his forehead to the bone. And Amykos lay stretched out on his back among the flower petals. When he regained his feet, the battle became fierce. The blows they aimed at one another were meant to kill. . . . Polydeuces the unbeaten pounded his opponent's whole face into a shapeless mass with disfiguring blows. . . . On the ground lay Amykos, all of him, with his wits wandering, and he held up both hands in surrender, for he was near death.

(in which people tossed up several tokens made of wood or bone and tried to catch them on the backs of their hands).

As was the case with the Greeks, some of the athletic games practiced by the Etruscans accompanied funerals and honored the dead. The events often included running contests, wrestling, boxing, discus throwing, and chariot races. In many ways they resembled the funeral games held for the Greek warrior Patroclus in the *Iliad*, the great epic poem by the Greek bard Homer. One difference is that the Etruscan versions of these events sometimes reveal an unusually strong interest in or appetite for dangerous and gory displays. The boxers wore leather thongs around their hands designed to cut and otherwise damage their opponents' faces. And charioteers tied their reins behind their backs so that if they crashed they could not jump free; they were therefore more likely to be badly injured or killed. There was also a very brutal game that is depicted in the so-called Tomb of the Augers, near Tarquinii, described here by Michael Grant:

> There is also a representation of [a man in a demon mask] launching a savage black dog at another man.

The victim of the attack, who wears an animal skin, holds a club to defend himself with, but is blindfolded, his head muffled in a bag. This scene may carry some [unknown] mythological meaning, but it has also been regarded [by many scholars] . . . as evidence of a cruel sort of Etruscan gladiatorial sport that foreshadowed the beast-fights of the Romans.[35]

In addition to athletic events, both bloody and nonbloody, the Etruscans practiced some of the same leisure sports that people enjoy today. Perhaps the most common were hunting and fishing. Several tomb paintings show these activities. One excellent example at Tarquinii, which scholars appropriately dubbed the Tomb of Hunting and Fishing, shows a boy fishing with a hook and line while sitting in a boat. Meanwhile, a man uses a slingshot in an attempt to shoot down some birds circling overhead. Scenes like this one remind modern viewers that, despite the vast rift of time, language, and culture that separates them from the Etruscans, in certain ways people in all times and places are, and always will be, the same.

CHAPTER SIX

THE CLASSICAL AGE: THE ETRUSCANS IN DECLINE

The period of Etruscan civilization that modern scholars call the Classical Age (ca. 480–ca. 300 B.C.) was an era in which the Etruscan city-states were severely tested against a wide range of strong and determined enemies. These opponents included the Greeks, the Samnites (members of a group of fierce tribes who inhabited the central Apennine Mountains), and the Gauls (intruders from the lands beyond the Alps). The Etruscans' most formidable adversary, however, was the rapidly expanding city-state of Rome. Time and again, Roman armies delivered Etruscan forces debilitating defeats.

This nineteenth-century woodcut shows Roman troops sacking the Etruscan stronghold of Veii in 396 B.C. In ensuing years, Rome overran all of Etruria.

To their credit, the Etruscans were a proud and resilient people. And they remained a potent force in Italian affairs throughout the nearly two centuries of the Classical Age. Yet the inability (or lack of desire) of the leading Etruscan states to unite played right into Roman hands and weakened these states collectively over time. The disastrous fall of Veii to Rome in the middle of the Classical Age signaled the beginning of the end of Etruria as a distinct and independent political and cultural sphere.

Etruscan Sea Power Wanes

Even as the Classical Age dawned, the Etruscans already found themselves in uncomfortable circumstances. On the positive side, they had recently undergone expansion, both northward toward the Po Valley and southward into Campania, where they had gained a strong foothold. But they had also suffered a series of reverses. In the late 500s B.C., a Greek army had routed the Campanian Etruscans near the Campanian town of Cumae, and a combined army of Greeks and Latins had crushed an Etruscan force from Clusium at Aricia, south of Rome.

Another blow against the Etruscans at the beginning of the Classical Age was indirect, yet still devastating. Aided by their allies, the Carthaginians, Etruscan ships had long dominated the waters lying between northern Italy and the islands of Sardinia and Corsica. In 480 B.C., however, this situation changed rather drastically. In that year Carthage launched a large war fleet in hopes of defeating the Greek cities of Sicily, especially Syracuse. (This offensive was timed to coincide with a Persian attack on mainland Greece, as the Persians and Carthaginians had recently formed an anti-Greek alliance.) Syracuse's leader, Gelon, decisively defeated the Carthaginian invasion force near the Sicilian town of Himera.

Gelon's victory forced the Carthaginians to withdraw and left the Etruscan naval forces without an ally. This was a significant development, for mastery of the sea in the region had become vital to Etruscan interests in Campania. The land route from Etruria to the Etruscan outposts in Campania had recently been blocked by the Romans and other Latins. This meant that the Campanian Etruscans were largely dependent on Etruscan naval forces for resupply, trade, and protection against the Campanian and Sicilian Greeks.

The seriousness of the growing plight of the Campanian Etruscans became even more apparent only a few years after the Carthaginian defeat at Himera. In 474 B.C., the Greeks at Cumae instigated a new conflict. They had been growing increasingly uncomfortable with the Etruscan presence in the region, so they asked the new leader of Syracuse, King Hiero I (Gelon's brother), to come to their aid. Hiero soon soundly defeated an Etruscan fleet near Cumae. This severely and permanently crippled Etruscan naval capacities in the region.

The Fall of Capua

The Greek victory also left the Campanian Etruscans in a precarious position, as they were now largely cut off from Etruria by both land and sea. Left for the most part to fend for themselves, they were unable to hold out long against the hostile forces that encircled them. Greeks occupied the lands on the southern flank of Campania and on the coast near Cumae. Meanwhile, Latin towns controlled Latium, situated north of Campania. And Samnite tribes inhabited the hills lying to the east and northeast.

About the year 423 B.C., the noose created by these peoples around the Campanian Etruscans tightened. Samnite forces entered Campania and captured Capua, the main Etruscan stronghold in the region. "The seizure of the town took place in particularly horrible circumstances," Livy wrote.

> The Samnites had been allowed by the Etruscans, whose strength had been drained by war, to share in the amenities of the town and in the working of the land belonging to it. One night, after a public holiday, when the native Etruscans were sleeping off the effects [of drinking too much], they [the Samnites] set upon them and butchered them.[36]

With the fall of Capua, the Etruscan presence in Campania could no longer be maintained. About two years later, the Samnites captured several other towns in the region that had recently been occupied by Etruscans, including Pompeii. The Samnites also took over Cumae from the local Greeks, forever ending that city's status as a major Italian power.

Veii and Rome at War

The loss of their Campanian associates was probably not a major blow to the leading city-states of Etruria. After all, for two generations the Etruscans of Etruria had been largely cut off from the Campanian Etruscans, who had been pretty much politically autonomous from the Etruscan heartland anyway. However, the states of that heartland were not immune to the

growing strength and aggressive moves of other Italian peoples.

The most serious threat to the Etruscan city-states was posed by Rome, situated on Etruria's southern edge about twelve miles from Veii's urban center. The wars between the Romans and Veientes, which lasted off and on for more than a century, in a way foreshadowed Rome's later and more extensive defeat and takeover of the whole of Etruria. In both cases, Roman successes were slowly paced and their gains often piecemeal. But the Romans were relentless and in the long run completely victorious.

Greek and Roman historians made brief mention of periodic troubles between the Romans and Veientes in the Etruscan Archaic Age. But these were likely minor squabbles, such as cattle raids. The major wars between the two city-states erupted in 480 B.C. at the opening of the Classical Age, and the same year that Gelon defeated the Carthaginians at Himera. At the time, Rome was suffering from internal dissensions among its social classes, as the common people (plebs) demanded increased political rights from the government, which was largely controlled by aristocrats. Evidently Veii's leaders, as well as the leaders of several other southern Etruscan states, saw their chance to take advantage of Rome's moment of weakness. And in a rare example of unity, they combined their forces. They hoped, Livy said, "that Rome might be destroyed by her internal dissensions." They also predicted that many Roman troops, who were plebs, would refuse to fight (as a way to press their political demands) and would even abandon their officers in the field. "Fate and the gods would do the rest. Such were the hopes which . . . induced the Etruscans to prepare once more for war."[37]

The large Etruscan army that assembled near Veii at first had the upper hand, at least psychologically. This is because the Roman commanders who marched out with their men to meet the enemy worried about the same thing that the Etruscans hoped for—that most of the Roman troops would not fight. So the Roman generals hesitated and for several days stayed in camp and refused to give battle. In response, Etruscan soldiers rode their horses close to the Roman tents and taunted the Romans, calling them cowards and a host of other insults. Eventually, though, this behavior backfired. According to Livy, it was

> too much for the Roman rank and file, who could endure such insolence no longer. . . . [There was] a noisy and spontaneous demonstration by the whole army. The time to strike had come. . . . Every man in the Roman army, roused to fury by the enemy's insults . . . entered the fight with a keener appetite for blood than in any previous campaign. The Etruscans were given no time to deploy [their troops in battle lines], before the Romans were upon them. . . . In less time than it takes to tell, the armies were locked in a struggle of the deadliest kind—sword against sword. . . . [The Etruscans] were cut to pieces, the survivors making off where and how they could.[38]

The Demise of Veii

Despite the high number of Etruscan casualties in the battle, Veii continued to oppose and threaten Rome. To protect their city, the members of a prominent and very wealthy

---

OTHER ETRUSCANS ABANDON VEII

The reasons why the other Etruscan cities did not help Veii during the great siege that led to the city's end remain somewhat unclear. All that survive are a few remarks by Greek and Roman historians suggesting that Veii's leader was not well liked in Etruria, including this passage by Livy (quoted in *Livy: The Early History of Rome*).

> The other Etruscan communities had taken offense . . . for personal reasons no less than for political [ones], as the man who was given supreme power in Veii [actually made king] had been generally disliked owing to his wealth and, more particularly, because of the outrage he had committed on their religious feelings by breaking up a solemn national festival. . . . The Etruscan communities, deeply learned as they were in sacred lore of all kinds, were more concerned than any other nation with religious matters, and for that reason they determined to refuse assistance to Veii while the king ruled there.

A seventeenth-century engraving depicts the Roman siege of Veii, which began in 405 B.C. Ten years later, the town fell.

Roman family, the Fabii, built a fort just seven miles from Veii. The Veientes viewed this move as an aggressive intrusion into their territory, and in 477 B.C. they ambushed and surrounded a group of some three hundred Fabii and other Romans near the fort. The trapped men fought valiantly but all were slain, except for one, who Livy said was "hardly more than a boy." He escaped and "survived to carry on the Fabian name,"[39] which was fortunate for Rome because the Fabii clan would later produce some important Roman leaders.

Emboldened by their minor victory over the Fabii, the Veientes speedily pushed southward and occupied the Janiculum Hill across the Tiber River from Rome. The Romans marched out to meet them and a bat-

tle took place only a mile from Rome. This was followed almost immediately by another fight very close to one of the city's gates. The Romans won both engagements, as well as another even larger one fought on the Janiculum the following year. The Veientes lost so many men in this battle that they were forced to retreat back to their own city.

Sporadic fighting between Rome and Veii continued in the years that followed, and over time the two peoples became increasingly bitter enemies. In Livy's words, they faced "each other with such mutual hatred and ferocity that none could doubt but that defeat for either would mean extinction."[40] Indeed, the Romans finally reached a point where they felt that Veii was simply too close for comfort, a menace that must be removed. According to Livy, a leading Roman legislator, Appius Claudius, gave the following justification for besieging, capturing, and if necessary eradicating the Etruscan city:

> Is our quarrel with Veii a slight one? . . . Come, come, on seven separate occasions they have started hostilities against us. In the intervals of peace we could never trust them. A thousand times they have devastated our farmlands . . . killed our settlers . . . and attempted to raise all Etruria against us. . . . Are those the sort of people we should fight with the gloves on? . . . Righteous indignation be enough to move us.

Veii should receive no mercy and no quarter, Claudius said, partly because Rome's future reputation was at stake:

> The terror of the Roman name will be such that the world shall know that, once a Roman army has laid siege to a city, nothing will move it . . . that it knows no end but victory and is ready, if a swift and sudden stroke will not serve, to persevere till that victory is achieved.[41]

Following this steadfast and ruthless policy, the Romans laid siege to Veii beginning about 405 B.C. It was no easy task. Like most other Etruscan urban centers, the town had sturdy defensive walls that were well designed to keep an enemy out. But the Romans persisted, month after month, year after year, steadily wearing down the inhabitants' resolve. Finally, in 396 B.C., the attackers completed a tunnel beneath the city's walls, and as Livy told it:

> In readiness for the decisive stroke, the tunnel had been filled with picked

Peter Connolly's reconstruction of ancient Veii, showing the fortified citadel in the foreground and the town sprawled behind it.

men, and now, without warning, it discharged them into the Temple of Juno [Uni to the Etruscans] on the citadel. The enemy, who were manning the walls against the threat from outside, were attacked from behind. Bolts were wrenched off the gates. Buildings were set on fire, as women and slaves on the roofs flung stones and tiles at the assailants. A fearful din arose: yells of triumph, shrieks of terror, the wailing of women, and the pitiful crying of children. In an instant of time the defenders were flung from the walls and the town gates opened; Roman troops came pouring through. . . . Everything was overrun, in every street the battle raged.[42]

Trouble in the North

Rome's victory was complete. In the following days, the Romans plundered the accumulated treasures of Veii, including the statues of its gods, and sold all surviving free Veientes into slavery. Rome also incorporated Veii's surrounding territory into the Roman city-state, nearly doubling its size. This first complete defeat and absorption of an Etruscan state by Rome marked an ominous precedent for the future of Etruria.

Moreover, the Romans were not the only enemy that posed a threat to that future. At the same time that Veii, on Etruria's southern flank, was falling to Rome, the Etruscan cities lying on Etruria's northern fringes and beyond also came under attack. In the last years of the fifth century B.C., the Gauls, a Celtic people from the areas now known as Switzerland and France, began migrating across the Alps. They came in waves, each wave dominated by one or more distinct

Gallic tribes. And they soon posed a potent threat to the Etruscan colonies in the southern Po Valley. Some ancient accounts said that one of these colonies fell to Gallic warriors on the very same day that, far to the south, the Romans breached Veii's walls. Soon afterward, the Etruscan settlements at Bologna and Marzabotto fell to the Gauls.

The threat to Etruria proper became real when a large Gallic army crossed the Apennines in 391 B.C. and moved on Clusium. "The plight of Clusium was a most alarming one," Livy wrote.

> Strange men in the thousands were at the gates, men the like of whom the townsfolk had never seen, outlandish warriors armed with strange weapons, who were rumored already to have scattered the Etruscan forces on both sides of the Po. It was a terrible situation.[43]

The immediate reaction of Clusium's leaders to the invaders is very revealing of the political situation in northern Italy at that time. One might expect that Clusium would call for aid from neighboring Etruscan cities—perhaps Cortona or Volsinii. Instead, however, Clusium appealed to Rome. This suggests that the leaders of Clusium were at the time not on good terms with their Etruscan neighbors; or that they felt these neighbors were not strong enough to deal with the Gauls; or that they recognized that Rome was the leading military power in the region; or in all likelihood all of these.

Rome responded by sending a delegation of prominent citizens, who met and tried to reason with the Gallic chieftains. The Gauls stated that this was the first they had ever heard of Rome. They were badly in need of land, they explained, and felt that Clusium had enough open territory that it should not object to ceding some of it to Gallic farmers. "You can have peace on no other terms"[44] was the final ultimatum delivered by the chieftains.

It was not long before tempers flared on both sides and a large-scale battle erupted between the Etruscans of Clusium and the invaders on their doorstep. At this juncture, the Roman envoys made what proved to be a fatal mistake. Even the illiterate and uncouth Gauls recognized the international rule that third-party peace negotiators were exempt from harm as long as they did not themselves take up arms. But the Roman envoys broke this rule by joining the Etruscans and even fighting in the front ranks of their army.

Because it was found in the town of Todi, this Etruscan bronze head of a warrior is called the "Mars of Todi."

This act enraged the Gauls. And following the engagement at Clusium (the outcome of which is unknown), they marched southward, bent on achieving revenge on Rome. In 390 B.C., a huge Gallic force confronted a hastily assembled group of mostly green Roman troops at the Allia River, north of Rome. The Romans suffered a shameful defeat and the intruders occupied the city briefly. (For many centuries to come, Roman calendars marked the date of the disaster as the "Day of Allia," a dark and unlucky day on which business should not be conducted nor trips initiated.) It is interesting that during this crisis the people of the Etruscan city of Caere offered the Romans aid. They sheltered Rome's priests and sacred objects, keeping them safe from the invaders, a kindness the Romans would later repay.

Roman Penetration of Etruria

Following their brief foray through Etruria, the Gauls returned to their main power base in the Po Valley and the Etruscans enjoyed a temporary respite from the threat in the north. However, the Etruscans were now tightly hemmed in between a permanent Gallic presence in the north, a Roman one in the south, and a Samnite one in the east. And all of these outside peoples looked inward on fertile Etruria as a valuable prize.

The Romans wasted no time in attempting to claim that prize. In the first half of the fourth century B.C., Rome made several aggressive moves into southern Etruria. Fighting was particularly intense between 358 and 351 B.C., with Caere, Tarquinii, and Falerii Veteres (situated northeast of Veii) the main Etruscan participants. The Etruscans consistently suffered reverses and in 353 Caere sued for peace. Likely in part to repay the favor the city had done the Romans after the disaster at Allia, Rome granted Caere a hundred-year truce. Two years later, a forty-year truce was negotiated between Rome and Tarquinii.

This seventeenth-century engraving shows Romans executing Etruscan soldiers after capturing their town. All Etruscan cities eventually fell to Rome.

THE ETRUSCANS DEFEATED AT SUTRIUM

This is Livy's description (quoted in *Livy: Rome and Italy*) of the first battle fought between the Etruscans and Romans before the city of Sutrium.

Midday passed and the sun began to sink before a missile was thrown from either side. Then the Etruscans, not wanting to leave the field with the issue unsettled, raised a battle-cry and sounded their trumpets as they charged forward. The Romans were no less eager to start fighting, and the two sides clashed in a furious encounter. The Etruscans were superior in numbers, the Romans in courage. The issue hung in the balance, and many fell on both sides, including all the bravest; nor was the result settled until the second Roman line came up fresh to the fight, to relieve the exhausted men in the front line, and the Etruscans, who had no fresh reserves to support their front line, all fell [dead] in front of their standards [flags and other symbols] and around them. . . . The signal for retreat was sounded after the sun had set, and in the night both armies returned to their camps.

The Etruscans and Romans faithfully observed the forty-year truce. However, in the meantime the first two of three wars between the Romans and Samnites took place. (The first war lasted from 343 to 341 B.C., the second from 326 to 304 B.C.) In 311 B.C., perhaps hoping to take advantage of Rome's vulnerability while it was engaged with the Samnites, armies from several Etruscan cities attacked a Roman ally, the city of Sutrium (southeast of Tarquinii). A Roman relief army arrived and a major and bitterly contested battle ensued. According to Livy:

The issue hung in the balance, and many fell on both sides, including all the bravest; nor was the result settled until the second Roman line came up fresh to the fight, to relieve the exhausted men in the front line, and the Etruscans, who had no fresh reserves to support their front line, all fell [dead] in front of their standards [flags and other symbols] and around them.[45]

Despite their defeat, the Etruscans did not give up their attempt to take Sutrium. It is probable that by now they had finally come to see that the Romans threatened their very existence as independent states. Since Veii had long since been absorbed into the Roman sphere, Sutrium had come to be seen, both geographically and symbolically, as the southern gateway to Etruria. And evidently the Etruscan view was that if Rome could be stopped at Sutrium, it could not penetrate any farther northward.

Whatever the Etruscans were thinking, in 310 B.C. they resumed their siege of Sutrium. Once more Rome sent a force to stop them, and this time the besiegers suffered an even bigger rout than before. The surviving Etruscans fled into a nearby forest that was known for being deep and treacherous. At first, most of the Roman troops were afraid to enter these woods. But not long afterward a Roman commander regrouped them, added reinforcements, and pushed deep into Etruria. After winning an unknown number of battles, the Romans forced the Etruscan cities of Perusia, Cortona, Arretium, and Tarquinii to sign treaties, the provisions of which strongly favored Rome.

In the years that followed, other Etruscan cities suffered military defeats at the hands of the Romans and had to sign humiliating treaties with the victors. In 298 B.C., at roughly the end of the Etruscan Classical Age, the Romans grappled with an Etruscan army near Volterrae. On the first day of fighting, both sides fought furiously until the sun's setting forced them to stop. The next morning, the Romans resumed the field to find that their opponents had fled during the night. In a way this retreat was symptomatic of and characterized the larger confrontation between the two peoples. It is unknown what the Etruscans themselves thought about the situation (although at the least they must have been deeply concerned). But the reality is clear enough in retrospect. Rome was rolling forward like an unstoppable force, and the days of an independent Etruria were clearly numbered.

THE END OF ETRUSCAN CIVILIZATION

Modern scholars call the final period of Etruscan history and culture the Hellenistic Age, which lasted from approximately 300 to 31 B.C. As this era opened, many of the Etruscan city-states were still intact. And some were still attempting to keep the Romans from overrunning Etruria. This resistance soon proved futile, however, and the people of Etruria had to face the reality that their days of proud autonomy were over.

Still, Roman military and political domination of Etruria did not immediately spell the end of Etruscan culture. In fact, many Etruscans managed to hold on to their cultural and artistic traditions, including their language, for several generations. The absorption of these traditions into the Roman cultural melting pot was a slow and uneven process. Yet it was dogged, unflinching, and unrelenting. And by the end of the first century B.C. it was more or less complete. As the Roman Republic collapsed and gave way to a new and more autocratic Roman political entity—the Empire—Etruscan language and culture had become quaint antiquities.

Last-Ditch Anti-Roman Alliances

To their credit, the Etruscans were in general persistent and brave and did not go down without a fight—in fact, numerous fights. In spite of repeated defeats at the hands of the Romans, Etruscan armies kept taking the field and trying to reverse the onrushing Roman tide that threatened to submerge all of Etruria. By the closing years of the Classical period, it must have become clear to most of the Etruscan states that they could no longer afford to fight Rome individually. Thus, Greek and Roman historians recorded a series of hastily assembled alliances among these states. For example, Livy pointed out that the Etruscan army that laid siege to Sutrium in 311 B.C. was composed of "all the peoples of Etruria, apart from the Arretini [people of Arretium]."[46]

In the early years of the Hellenistic Age, as the Etruscans' situation grew increasingly desperate, they also attempted to foil Rome by forming alliances with former enemies. In particular, these included the Gauls and Samnites. Rome had defeated the Samnites a second time, ending the Second Samnite War in 304 B.C. But only six years later the Samnites instigated a third war with Rome, and this time the Etruscans and Gauls, as well as the Umbrians (who lived in the eastern Apennines), aided the Samnites. It appears that these four peoples were confident that their combined might would be enough to destroy Rome once and for all.

It was a vain hope, however. For the Etruscans, the major turning point in the war occurred at Sentinum, in Umbria (in eastern Italy), in 295 B.C. According to Livy:

A day was fixed for the battle, the Samnites and Gauls were chosen to engage in it, and during the actual fighting the Etruscans and Umbrians were to attack the Roman camp. These plans were upset by three [Etr-

This bronze statuette of a man offering a sacrifice was made during Etruria's Hellenistic Age (ca. 300–31 B.C.).

uscan] deserters from Clusium, who came over [to the Romans] secretly by night . . . and [revealed] the enemy's intentions.

The Roman commanders wisely sent messengers to Roman forces stationed in Etruria. And these forces immediately launched an attack on Clusium, destroying its villages and farmlands "with the utmost vigor." This approach had the desired effect, for "the devastation they carried out was reported to the Etruscans, who then withdrew from the region of Sentinum in order to defend their own territories."[47]

With the Etruscans gone and the secret plan known to the Roman commanders, the remaining allies at Sentinum were at a severe disadvantage and were soundly defeated. Rome went on to mount a full-scale invasion of the Samnites' mountain heartland. And by 290 B.C. the once mighty Samnites had been permanently eliminated as a leading Italian power. The Etruscans and Gauls kept up the fight for a while. But their alliance suffered a major defeat near Lake Vadimo (about fifty miles north of Rome) in 282 B.C.

Etruria Slowly Reshaped

This Roman victory seems to have been more or less a turning point in the long Roman-Etruscan struggle for supremacy in Etruria. From about 280 B.C. on, it appears that Rome had the upper

A painting by Peter Paul Rubens depicts the battle of Sentinum in 295 B.C., which Rome won.

hand and controlled the region. Most of the Etruscan city-states still existed and continued for the most part to administer their own internal affairs. But in the larger political sphere they were no longer completely independent nation-states.

Instead, the Etruscan states had become subject-allies of Rome. This meant that they could form no alliances with other peoples and states without Rome's permission. Also, they could no longer maintain their own armies. All Etruscan men of a certain age were thereafter required to serve in the Roman army in divisions known as the *alae sociorum*, or "wings of allies." These soldiers, along with most other Etruscans, were not Roman citizens and therefore did not enjoy the many civil rights accorded citi-

zens. One possible exception were the inhabitants of Caere, some of whom may have received citizenship as early as the 300s B.C. (perhaps another reward for the favor they did Rome in 390).

As time went on, Rome not only exercised military and political control over Etruria but also slowly, in small but meaningful increments, reshaped it physically and culturally. This was not part of a long-range and sinister Roman plan. Rather, it was the inevitable long-range result of steadily changing times, a series of isolated policies and events, and the natural progression of both Roman and Etruscan civilizations.

For example, during the third century B.C., Rome periodically manipulated Etruscan lands and populations at will. This

These ruins are the remains of an Etruscan town that became Romanized, the fate of most of the once independent Etruscan cities.

began to upset the ancient and traditional political and social order in Etruria. One way this happened was when the Roman government established colonies (*coloniae* in Latin) in Etruscan territories and settled Roman citizens in these colonies. Archaeologists have excavated parts of one such colony founded in 273 B.C. at Cosa, in the territory of Vulci. "Like all Roman *coloniae*," Barker and Rasmussen explain,

> it was laid out like a small but more regularized version of Rome itself, with a forum [town square] area surrounded by public buildings and with a temple to the Roman state gods. . . . The precise number of original colonists is not known—one informed guess puts it at 2,500 adult males, which together with all family members would

make a total figure of about 9,000. But Cosa itself was too small a site to have accommodated all of them. Some would have been settled on farms allocated to them in the surrounding area. . . . [Rome's] landless poor were in this way enabled to make a new start with an allotment of land, but only at the expense of the recently vanquished, in this case the [local] Etruscans.[48]

Indeed, it appears that the people of Vulci lost as much as a third of their traditional territory in only the first decade following their final defeat by Rome. Other Etruscan states suffered similarly. Even Caere, which enjoyed the friendliest relations with Rome of any Etruscan city in this period, was not immune. Some evidence suggests that the Romans had confiscated nearly half of Caere's territory by 270 B.C. During this stage of colonization, the Romans were careful to take over the old Etruscan ports, as well as establish new ones. This ensured that the Etruscan states would no longer be able to maintain overseas trade; they would hereafter be increasingly dependent on Roman merchants for many vital goods, especially imported luxury items.

Forced Relocations and the Effects of Civil War

Another Roman tactic that helped to reshape Etruria over time was the occasional forced removal of entire Etruscan popula-

tions from their ancestral towns or lands. In 265 B.C., for instance, Rome moved all of the residents of Volsinii's urban center off their hilltop location and settled them on the shore of Lake Bolsena. In a similar manner, in 241 B.C. the Etruscans of Falerii Veteres were relocated to a less defensible site in southern Etruria.

Such population removals can be compared in many ways with the forced relocation of several American Indian tribes by the U.S. government in the nineteenth century. These tribes were devastated. Their members had to make new lives for themselves in strange regions far from the only homes they had known and on lands that were usually

The Roman military strongman Lucius Cornelius Sulla attacks his enemies in Rome. Sulla also besieged several Etruscan cities.

far less productive than those they originally owned. Uprooted Etruscans must have suffered in at least some of the same ways.

For about two centuries, the deprivations of Roman colonization and confiscation of Etruscan lands were confined mainly to the southern half of Etruria. In the north, no Roman colonies were established between Vulci and the Arno River before the first century B.C. Perhaps because they had the good fortune to be located farther away from Rome, for a while the northern Etruscan cities were granted treaties. These agreements stipulated that said cities were subject to and dependent on Rome. But at least their lands remained largely intact.

In the first century B.C., however, this situation changed, mainly because of a civil war waged between the forces of the Roman military strongmen Marius and Sulla. Most of the northern Etruscan cities sided with Marius. And in retaliation Sulla besieged and badly damaged some, including Populonia and Volterrae. In addition, Sulla settled thousands of his army veterans on the lands of these cities, driving untold thousands of Etruscans from their homes. At least some of the refugees left Italy entirely. Evidence has been found that dispossessed Etruscans from Clusium sailed to Tunisia, in North Africa, and tried to create a new community there. (For reasons unknown, the town disappeared after no more than a few generations.)

Striking Displays of Wealth and Loyalty

In spite of their steady decline and loss of territory and population, the Etruscan cities

The Carthaginian general Hannibal rides an elephant in a victory parade. Hannibal failed to convince the Etruscans to join his fight against Rome.

remained economically viable for some time. This is proven by the part they played in the Second Punic War, fought between Rome and Carthage from 218 to 201 B.C. When the Roman general Publius Cornelius Scipio was preparing to invade North Africa in 205 B.C., various Italian cities allied to Rome volunteered supplies. And according to Livy:

> The peoples of Etruria were the first to promise aid . . . in proportion to their respective means. Caere offered grain for the [ship] crews and supplies of all sorts; Populonia promised iron; Tarquinia sail-cloth; Volterrae grain and timber; . . . Arretium 3,000 shields, 3,000 helmets, and a total of 50,000 pikes, javelins, and spears . . . together with enough axes, shovels, sickles, basins, and hand-mills, to equip forty warships; also 120,000 measures of wheat and a contribution towards traveling allowances of petty officers and oarsmen. Perusia, Clusium, and Rusellae offered fir for building and a large quantity of grain.[49]

Even more striking than the economic wealth still possessed by these cities is the fact that they were so willing to aid and supply the Romans, who had treated them so badly in recent memory. Indeed, the conquered Etruscans demonstrated their loyalty to Rome in other ways as well. When the legendary Carthaginian general Hannibal invaded Italy earlier in the same conflict, part of his plan was to get Rome's subject allies to defect to his side. Incredibly, the Etruscan cities (along with most of Rome's other Italian allies) refused to join him. The Etruscans also helped the Romans perma-nently defeat the last remnants of Gallic armies in northern Italy in the late third century B.C.

The Survival of the Fittest

As for why the Etruscans were so helpful to Rome in this era, the ancient sources are silent. Perhaps they did so out of fear that the Romans would confiscate even more of their lands. It is also possible that Etruscan leaders had reconciled themselves to their subjugation and decided to make the best of their situation. In that case, they may have reasoned that what was good for Rome in the greater scheme of things was also good for them. In fact, some evidence suggests that, in exchange for such shows of loyalty, at least some Etruscans were rewarded with Roman citizenship. This would have allowed them to retain ownership of their family lands. And modern studies of the Tuscan countryside do indicate that significant numbers of rural Etruscans kept working their farms right up to the end of the Republic and beyond.

The question, however, is how long these farmers and those Etruscans who lived in cities continued to think of themselves as Etruscans. Attainment of Roman citizenship, intermarriage with Romans, and the ongoing adoption of Roman customs and ideas slowly but surely diluted traditional Etruscan culture. At the same time, increasing numbers of Etruscans grew up speaking Latin as their first language and Etruscan as their second, with fewer Etruscan speakers in each new generation. As the decades and centuries passed, more and more Etruscans came to think of themselves as "Romans of Etruscan descent" rather than simply as Etruscans. (In a similar manner, most citizens

These tomb images of Etruscans serve as reminders that all human civilizations, no matter how splendid, eventually pass away.

of the United States define themselves as Americans of Italian, English, Spanish, African, or some other descent.)

By the first century A.D., at the dawn of the Roman Empire, this slow process of assimilation was more or less complete. As Ellen Macnamara puts it: "Etruscan art and civilization had merged with that of Imperial Rome."[50] A handful of people in remote villages still kept the Etruscan language alive for a century or more to come. And some priests in Etruria continued to pass on the old skills of reading the future in lightning flashes and animals' livers.

But for all intents and purposes, the Etruscans of old were no more. In a process that has, for good or ill, been repeated endlessly throughout history, one of the greatest civilizations of the ancient world had been totally absorbed by one that had been stronger, more unified, and more determined. In that respect, the raw and pitiless doctrine of the survival of the fittest had proved the Etruscans' ultimate undoing.

Notes

Introduction: Lifting the Veil of Mystery

1. J.H. Breasted, *Ancient Times: A History of the Early World*, Boston: Ginn, 1944, pp. 312, 314, 570–71. For several years this book was one of the most widely read ancient history texts in American colleges.
2. Graeme Barker and Tom Rasmussen, *The Etruscans*. Malden, MA: Blackwell, 2000, pp. 3–4.
3. Michael Grant, *The Etruscans*. New York: Scribners, 1980, pp. 1–2.
4. *Quest for the Past*. Pleasantville, NY: Reader's Digest, 1984, p. 93.
5. Nigel Spivey, *Etruscan Art*. London: Thames and Hudson, 1997, p. 196.

Chapter 1: Origins and Development of Etruscan Culture

6. Hesiod, *Theogony*, in *Hesiod and Theognis*, trans. Dorothea Wender. New York: Penguin, 1973, p. 56.
7. Herodotus, *The Histories*, trans. Aubrey de Sélincourt. New York: Penguin, 1972, pp. 80–81.
8. Dionysius of Halicarnassus, *The Roman Antiquities*, trans. Ernest Cary. 7 vols. Cambridge, MA: Harvard University Press, 1963, vol. 1, p. 85.
9. Ellen Macnamara, *The Etruscans*. Cambridge, MA: Harvard University Press, 1991, p. 11.
10. Barker and Rasmussen, *Etruscans*, p. 83.

11. Barker and Rasmussen, *Etruscans*, p. 53.
12. Macnamara, *Etruscans*, pp. 8–9.
13. Grant, *Etruscans*, pp. 37–39.

Chapter 2: The Rapid Rise of the Etruscan City-States

14. Barker and Rasmussen, *Etruscans*, p. 118.
15. Barker and Rasmussen, *Etruscans*, p. 123.
16. Macnamara, *Etruscans*, p. 17.
17. Livy, *The History of Rome from Its Foundation*, books 1–5 published as *Livy: The Early History of Rome*, trans. Aubrey de Sélincourt. New York: Penguin, 1960, pp. 72–73.
18. Barker and Rasmussen, *Etruscans*, p. 126.

Chapter 3: The Etruscans at the Height of Their Power

19. Grant, *Etruscans*, p. 121.
20. Barker and Rasmussen, *Etruscans*, p. 260.
21. Livy, *Early History of Rome*, p. 121.
22. T.J. Cornell, *The Beginnings of Rome: Italy and Rome from the Bronze Age to the Punic Wars (c. 1000–264 B.C.)*. London: Routledge, 1995, p. 155.

Chapter 4: Etruscan Culture, Arts, and Crafts

23. Ellen Macnamara, *Everyday Life of the Etruscans*, New York: Dorset, 1987, p. 62.
24. Macnamara, *Everyday Life*, pp. 74–75.
25. Barker and Rasmussen, *Etruscans*, p. 97.
26. Grant, *Etruscans*, p. 64.
27. Barker and Rasmussen, *Etruscans*, p. 229.

28. Vitruvius, *On Architecture*, trans. Morris H. Morgan. Cambridge, MA: Harvard University Press, 1914, p. 122.
29. Spivey, *Etruscan Art*, p. 38.
30. Macnamara, *Etruscans*, p. 34.

Chapter 5: Etruscan Homes, Society, and Leisure Activities

31. Quoted in Elaine Fantham et al., *Women in the Classical World*. New York: Oxford University Press, 1994, p. 248.
32. Macnamara, *Everyday Life*, p. 169.
33. Livy, *The History of Rome from Its Foundation*, books 6–10 published as *Livy: Rome and Italy*, trans. Betty Radice. New York: Penguin, 1982, p. 293.
34. Livy, *Rome and Italy*, pp. 98–99.
35. Grant, *Etruscans*, p. 128.

Chapter 6: The Classical Age: The Etruscans in Decline

36. Livy, *Rome and Italy*, pp. 309–10.

37. Livy, *Early History of Rome*, p. 156.
38. Livy, *Early History of Rome*, pp. 159–60.
39. Livy, *Early History of Rome*, p. 165.
40. Livy, *Early History of Rome*, p. 341.
41. Livy, *Early History of Rome*, pp. 345, 347.
42. Livy, *Early History of Rome*, p. 365.
43. Livy, *Early History of Rome*, pp. 380–81.
44. Livy, *Early History of Rome*, p. 381.
45. Livy, *Rome and Italy*, p. 362.

Epilogue: The End of Etruscan Civilization

46. Livy, *Rome and Italy*, p. 261.
47. Livy, *Rome and Italy*, pp. 326–27.
48. Barker and Rasmussen, *Etruscans*, p. 262.
49. Livy, *The History of Rome from Its Foundation*, books 21–30 published as *Livy: The War with Hannibal*, trans. Aubrey de Sélincourt. New York: Penguin, 1972, p. 562.
50. Macnamara, *Etruscans*, p. 59.

Chronology

B.C.

ca. 2000–ca. 900
Approximate years of the Bronze Age in Etruria (today called Tuscany), the Etruscan heartland, lying north of Rome.

ca. 900–ca. 700
Years of the Iron Age in Etruria, also referred to as the Villanovan period after the first archaeological finds of Etruscan iron artifacts discovered in a cemetery near the Italian town of Villanova.

753
Traditional date for the founding of Rome (according to ancient Roman scholars); however, archaeology shows that the site of Rome was occupied at least two centuries earlier.

ca. 700–ca. 600
The Orientalizing Period of Etruria, in which eastern Mediterranean influences, especially Greek ones, have profound effects on Etruscan culture.

ca. 650
A richly decorated palacelike structure (uncovered in the twentieth century by archaeologists) is built by one or more Etruscan aristocrats at Murlo, near the major Etruscan city of Volterrae.

ca. 600–ca. 480
The Archaic Age of Etruria, in which the Etruscans expand their interests both northward and southward and reach their height of power.

ca. 535
A combined Etruscan and Carthaginian fleet defeats the Phocaean Greeks in a sea battle fought near the island of Corsica.

ca. 509
The leading Roman landowners lock their Etruscan-born king outside the city, dissolve the kingship, and establish the Roman Republic.

ca. 506

An Etruscan army from Clusium is defeated by an allied army of Greeks and Latins at Aricia, south of Rome.

ca. 480–ca. 300

The Classical Age of Etruria, in which Etruscan armies repeatedly suffer defeat and Etruscan civilization steadily declines in power and prestige.

480

The Etruscans' allies, the Carthaginians, are defeated by the Greek city of Syracuse near Himera, in Sicily; hostilities break out between the Etruscan city of Veii and Rome.

477

Soldiers from Veii surround and slaughter a contingent of Romans about seven miles south of Veii; several more battles ensue in the months that follow, one fought near one of Rome's gates.

474

An Etruscan fleet is defeated near Cumae by a Syracusan fleet.

423

Capua, the leading Etruscan town of the fertile region of Campania, falls to the Samnites.

396

After a long siege, Veii falls to Rome, which absorbs the defeated city's territory.

391

The city of Clusium is threatened by a large army of Gauls from the Po Valley (in northern Italy).

390

The Gauls march southward through Etruria, defeat a Roman army near the Allia River, and briefly occupy Rome.

353

After several years of fighting the Romans, the Etruscan city of Caere signs a hundred-year truce with Rome.

326–304

Years of the Second Samnite War (as the Romans called it), during which the Etruscans try to take advantage of Rome's preoccupation with fighting the Samnites.

311
An Etruscan army besieges the town of Sutrium, a Roman ally, but is defeated by a Roman relief force.

ca. 300–ca. 31
The Hellenistic Age of Etruria, in which the Etruscan cities and their cultures are slowly but steadily absorbed into the greater Roman melting pot.

298
The Romans defeat the Etruscans near Volterrae.

282
The Etruscans suffer another defeat at the hands of the Romans near Lake Vadimo (fifty miles north of Rome).

273
The Romans establish a colony at Cosa, in the territory of the Etruscan state of Vulci. Over time, more and more Roman settlers displace Etruscan landowners and farmers.

A.D.

Early first century
By this time, with a few scattered exceptions, Etruscan culture has been totally absorbed by Roman civilization.

FOR FURTHER READING

Books

Marilynn G. Barr, *Etruscans*. Carthage, IL: Teach Learning, 2002. This simplified overview of Etruscan civilization is aimed at basic readers.

Dale M. Brown, ed., *Etruscans: Italy's Lovers of Life*. New York: Time-Life, 1995. A colorful general introduction to Etruscan civilization for general readers, with numerous attractive photos of Tuscany.

Don Nardo, *From Founding to Fall: A History of Rome*. San Diego: Lucent, 2003. A readable, useful general overview of Roman history, providing a framework for understanding the relationship between the Etruscans and Romans.

Judith Simpson, *Ancient Rome*. New York: Time-Life, 1997. Another of Time-Life's library of picture books about the ancient world, this one is beautifully illustrated with attractive photographs and paintings.

Web Sites

Ars Haruspicina (www.cs.utk.edu/~mclennan/OM/BA/Har.html). A fascinating review of the Etruscan art and practice of divination.

Discovery Channel, "Clients and Patrons," (http://myron.sjsu.edu/romeweb/SOCIAL/art2.htm). An excellent overview of the Roman social system of patronage. It now seems certain that the Etruscans had a very similar system.

Etruscan Language (www.mysteriousetruscans.com/language.html). An easy to understand introduction to what is known about the Etruscan language, which was unlike any other in ancient Europe.

Etruscan Liber Linteus (http://users.tpg.com.au/etr/etrusk/default.html). An excellent site that dissects and discusses the only surviving long Etruscan inscription, found in the 1800s in a mummy wrapping in Egypt.

In Search of the Etruscan (www.premier.net/~Italy/etrus-htm). A helpful tour of some of the more important Etruscan archaeological sites.

WORKS CONSULTED

Major Works

Graeme Barker and Tom Rasmussen, *The Etruscans*. Malden, MA: Blackwell, 2000. One of the best recent overviews of Etruscan civilization, with many useful maps and charts.

Larissa Bonfante, *Etruscan*. Berkeley and Los Angeles: University of California Press, 1990. In this volume, Bonfante, one of the leading modern scholars of the Etruscans, examines the Etruscan language, which has not yet been fully deciphered.

Larissa Bonfante and Judith Swaddling, *Etruscan Myths*. Austin: University of Texas Press, 2004. This fine new book looks at what is known about the myths of the Etruscans and how they were influenced by those of the Greeks.

T.J. Cornell, *The Beginnings of Rome: Italy and Rome from the Bronze Age to the Punic Wars (c. 1000–264 B.C.)*. London: Routledge, 1995. Contains considerable useful information about the Etruscans and their influences on the early Romans. Cornell here defends the thesis that the Etruscans did not conquer Rome.

Michael Grant, *The Etruscans*. New York: Scribners, 1980. Though now a bit dated, this study of the Etruscans by a major scholar remains a valuable overview, with many detailed descriptions of archaeological sites and artifacts.

Sybille Haynes, *Etruscan Civilization: A Cultural History*. Los Angeles: J. Paul Getty Museum, 2000. A well-mounted scholarly look at the Etruscans.

Ellen Macnamara, *The Etruscans*. Cambridge, MA: Harvard University Press, 1991. The distinguished British Museum scholar presents an excellent brief overview of Etruscan civilization, with an emphasis on archaeological evidence, especially arts and crafts.

———, *Everyday Life of the Etruscans*. New York: Dorset, 1987. In this longer volume, Macnamara attempts to reconstruct everyday Etruscan life through the sometimes scant archaeological evidence.

Massimo Pallottino, *The Etruscans*. Harmondsworth, England: Penguin, 1975. Scholars consider this book the classic modern description of the Etruscans. Where needed, its information was updated in the 1980s and 1990s by Pallottino and others.

H.H. Scullard, *The Etruscan Cities and Rome*. Baltimore: Johns Hopkins University Press, 1998. A reprint of Scullard's older study of the Etruscan cities. Still an informational and useful book.

Nigel Spivey, *Etruscan Art*. London: Thames and Hudson, 1997. Spivey, the great British ancient-art historian, has compiled a first-rate overview of Etruscan culture and art, with many excellent color and black-and-white photos.

Other Important Works

Primary Sources

Dionysius of Halicarnassus, *The Roman Antiquities*. Trans. Ernest Cary. 7 vols. Cambridge, MA: Harvard University Press, 1963.

Herodotus, *The Histories*. Trans. Aubrey de Sélincourt. New York: Penguin, 1972.

Hesiod, *Theogony*, in *Hesiod and Theognis*. Trans. Dorothea Wender. New York: Penguin, 1973.

Livy, *The History of Rome from Its Foundation*, books 1–5 published as *Livy: The Early History of Rome*. Trans. Aubrey de Sélincourt. New York: Penguin, 1960; books 6–10 published as *Livy: Rome and Italy*. Trans. Betty Radice. New York: Penguin, 1982; books 21–30 published as *Livy: The War with Hannibal*. Trans. Aubrey de Sélincourt. New York: Penguin, 1972.

Jo-Ann Shelton, ed., *As the Romans Did: A Sourcebook in Roman Social History*. New York: Oxford University Press, 1988.

Waldo E. Sweet, ed., *Sport and Recreation in Ancient Greece: A Sourcebook with Translations*. New York: Oxford University Press, 1987.

Vitruvius, *On Architecture*. Trans. Morris H. Morgan. Cambridge, MA: Harvard University Press, 1914.

Modern Sources

Paul G. Bahn, ed., *The Cambridge Illustrated History of Archaeology*. New York: Cambridge University Press, 1996.

J.D. Beazley, *Etruscan Vase Painting*. Oxford, England: Clarendon, 1947.

Larissa Bonfante, *Etruscan Dress*. Baltimore: Johns Hopkins University Press, 2003.

Giovanni P. Carratelli, *The Western Greeks*. Milan: Bompiani, 1996.

Peter Connolly, *Greece and Rome at War*. London: Macdonald, 1998.

Jean-Michel David, *The Roman Conquest of Italy*. Trans. Antonia Nevill. London: Blackwell, 1996.

Elaine Fantham et al., *Women in the Classical World*. New York: Oxford University Press, 1994.

Sybille Haynes, *Etruscan Bronzes*. London: Sotheby's, 1985.

R.R. Holloway, *The Archaeology of Early Rome and Latium*. New York: Routledge, 1994.

Georg Luck, *Arcana Mundi: Magic and the Occult in the Greek and Roman Worlds*. Baltimore: Johns Hopkins University Press, 1985.

Paul MacKendrick, *The Mute Stones Speak: The Story of Archaeology in Italy*. New York: St. Martin's, 1960.

Kyle M. Philips Jr., *In the Hills of Tuscany: Recent Excavations at the Etruscan Site of Poggio Civitate*. Philadelphia: University of Pennsylvania Museum, 1993.

Tom Rasmussen, *Bucchero Pottery from Southern Etruria*. Cambridge, England: Cambridge University Press, 1979.

INDEX

Carthaginians, 46, 77, 93

Cerveteri. See Caere

chariot racing, 75

Charun (demon), 56

Chiusi. *See* Clusium

cities and towns, 22, 24, 29–32, 34

Classical Age

  clothing, 72

  fall of Capua, 77–78

  sea power, 77

  war with Gauls, 82–84

  war with Rome, 78–82, 84–86

Claudius, Appius, 81

climate, 19–20

clothing, 25, 70–72

Clusium (city), 32, 82–83, 88

Collatinus, Lucius Tarquinius, 50

colonies, Roman, 90

Connolly, Peter, 43

copper, 21

Cornell, T.J., 47

Cortona, 32

cottabos (game), 74

crafts. *See* arts and crafts

cremation, 23, 28

Cumae, battle near, 47

dancing, 73–74

demons, 56

Dionysius (Greek historian), 17

disunity, 39–41

divination, 55, 94

employment, 69–70

entertainment, 72–75

eras, 20–21

Etruscan people

  migrations of, 39, 91

  names of, 15

  origins of, 14–18, 22

Etruscans, The (Macnamara), 60

expansion, 46–47, 77

Fabii family, 80

Faesulae (city), 32, 34

farms, 19–20, 65

fasces (weapon), 65–66

field walking, 31–32

fishing, 75

freedmen, 69–70

funerals, 28, 75

games, 74–75

Gauls, 82–84, 87, 88

Gelon (leader of Syracuse), 77

gods and goddesses, 54–55, 57

government, 40–41, 65–67

  Bronze Age, 21

  Roman, 78

Grant, Michael, 11, 25, 35, 41, 55, 75

Greece and Rome at War (Connolly), 43

Greek influence

  in Archaic Age, 41–45

  in arts and crafts, 51–52, 60

  in clothing, 71–72

  in housing, 63

  in Orientalizing Period, 34–38

  in religion, 54–56

PICTURE CREDITS

ABOUT THE AUTHOR

Historian and award-winning writer Don Nardo has published many books about the ancient world, including *Life in Ancient Athens; Life of a Roman Gladiator; Egyptian Mythology; Empires of Mesopotamia;* literary companions to the works of Homer, Sophocles, and Euripides; and the *Greenhaven Encyclopedia of Greek and Roman Mythology*. He lives with his wife, Christine, in Massachusetts.